At Issue

Is Poverty a Serious Threat?

Other books in the At Issue series:

At Issue

Is Poverty a Serious Threat?

Mercedes Muñoz, Book Editor

GREENHAVEN PRESS

An imprint of Thomson Gale, a part of The Thomson Corporation

THOMSON
™
GALE

Detroit • New York • San Francisco • San Diego • New Haven, Conn.
Waterville, Maine • London • Munich

For more information, contact:
Greenhaven Press
27500 Drake Rd.
Farmington Hills, MI 48331-3535
Or you can visit our Internet site at http://www.gale.com

LIBRARY OF CONGRESS CATALOGING-IN-PUBLICATION DATA

Is poverty a serious threat? / Mercedes Muñoz, book editor.
   p. cm. -- (At Issue)
   Includes bibliographical references and index.
   ISBN 0-7377-2725-X (lib. bdg. : alk. paper) -- ISBN 0-7377-2726-8
(pbk. : alk. paper)
1. Poverty--United States. 2. Poor--United States. 3. Income distribution--United States. 4. United States--Economic conditions--2001~5. United States--Social conditions--1980~
I. Muñoz, Mercedes. II. At issue (San Diego, Calif.)
   HC110.P6I8 2006
   362.50973--dc22

                                                        2005054523

Printed in the United States of America
10 9 8 7 6 5 4 3 2 1

Contents

Introduction

In September 2005 television images of poor residents trapped by floodwaters in New Orleans, Louisiana, in the wake of Hurricane Katrina, raised questions about the extent and seriousness of poverty in the United States. Yet one of the issues surrounding the topic of poverty, both in the United States and elsewhere, is a lack of agreement on what, exactly, poverty is.

Although different countries define poverty in different ways, the World Bank uses a standard definition to facilitate comparisons among nations. This measure defines extreme poverty as living on less than one dollar a day; more than 1 billion people worldwide are considered poor using this definition. An additional 3 billion people live on less than two dollars per day. Many experts, however, say that income level alone is too conservative a measure of poverty, and that factors such as access to healthcare, education, clean water, and adequate housing should also be taken into account. They argue as well that economic inequality—the gap between rich and poor within a nation and among nations—is an important indicator of poverty that is absent from measures that rely solely on income levels. Economist Martin Ravallion explains: "While one could hardly argue that the people in the world who are poor by the standards typical of the poorest countries are not in fact poor, there are many more people in the world who are poor by the standards of middle-income countries." Many economists such as John Kenneth Galbraith believe that when individuals or groups have far less money and material goods than do others within the same society, they feel poor even if, by official reckoning, they are not. Galbraith argues, "People are poverty-stricken when their income, even if adequate for survival, falls radically behind that of the community."

Despite concerns about defining poverty by income level alone, income (apart from noncash benefits provided by government entitlement programs such as Medicaid) is the primary measure by which poverty is defined in the United States. Moreover, the formula by which the poverty threshold is defined, developed by economist Mollie Orshansky as part of President Lyndon Johnson's War on Poverty, has remained unchanged since it was adopted in 1965. In 2005 the poverty line used by the Department of Health and Human Services was $19,350 per year for a family of four.

Many critics argue that the poverty line should be redrawn because the measurements by which Orshansky defined it forty years ago do not reflect today's economic realities. Her calculations were based on the fact that at the time, an average family of three or more spent one-third of its budget on food. Today, however, the Council of Economic Advisers estimates that the average American family spends only 14 percent of its budget on food.

Lower food costs, however, have been offset by greater expenses in other areas. One of these is health-care costs. Declining rates of employer-paid health insurance have meant that medical costs often consume a larger proportion of a poor family's budget than was true in 1965. James Mullahy and Barbara L. Wolfe, professors at the University of Wisconsin-Madison, write, "Since the late 1970s there has been a steady drop in the proportion of private-sector workers with employer-sponsored coverage, especially among the lowest-paid workers, whose coverage rates dropped by nearly 25 percent between 1987 and 1996." The cost of housing, too, has increased: The American Housing Survey estimated that in 2003, the typical household in poverty spent 64 percent of its income for housing.

The fact that the proportion of income that the poor spend on various items has changed so radically since Orshansky arrived at her original formula has raised the question of whether the U.S. government's definition of poverty is realistic today. This question is a crucial one for many. Up to two hundred federal programs use the guidelines to determine who is eligible for assistance, including the Women, Infants, and Children (WIC) supplemental nutrition plan; food stamps; Medicaid; and Temporary Assistance to Needy Families (TANF). Many critics argue that the U.S. poverty level is so low that it excludes many families who desperately need help from getting it.

Yet other critics of the U.S. poverty threshold denounce it for a different reason. They say the very fact that the guidelines do not count government entitlement benefits as income artificially inflates the number of people under the poverty line. If these benefits, such as food stamps and Medicaid, were included as income, they say, far fewer people could be considered to be impoverished. These critics also argue that the government's definition of poverty does not take into account the relatively comfortable lifestyle of the poor in the United States. Robert E. Rector of the Heritage Foundation, for example, writes: "Overall, the typical American defined as poor by the government has a car, air conditioning, a refrigerator, a stove, a clothes washer and dryer, and a microwave. . . . While this individual's life is not opulent, it is equally far from the popular images of dire poverty conveyed by the press, activists and politicians."

With such disparate views of what constitutes poverty and whether it is a serious problem, it is unlikely that there will be widespread agreement on these issues in the foreseeable future. Still, ongoing dialogue about the subject may lead to more common ground about who the poor really are and what, if anything, should be done to help them.

1

The Poor Are Worse Off in the United States than in Other Countries

David R. Francis

David R. Francis is a reporter for The Christian Science Monitor.

While upper- and middle-class Americans do well compared with upper- and middle-class citizens of other industrialized nations, America's poor do not. This is because the United States has worse income distribution—in other words, there are vast differences in the incomes of people at various economic levels. Moreover, there is no safety net to address these inequities as there is in other nations. This situation puts low-income American children at a disadvantage.

Except for the citizens of a few tiny oil kingdoms and Luxembourg, Americans on average live better than anybody else.

Germans? Forget it. Americans' standard of living is 30 percent higher. The British? The gap's even wider.

But if the United States is so rich, critics ask, how come its poor are poorer than almost anywhere else in the developed world?

Consider Canada. Its median per capita gross domestic product (GDP), that is, the output of goods and services for the typical Canadian, is 19 percent below the median in the U.S. Nevertheless, the poorest 18 percent of Canadians remain better off, on average, than the poorest 18 percent of Americans.

The contrast is even starker in oil-rich Norway, where the poorest 38 percent of the people fare better, on average, than the poorest 38 percent of Americans, despite a lower median per capita GDP.

The reason? America's woefully unequal distribution of income. . . .

Income Distribution in America

The US has the worst distribution of income of any well-to-do country. In a list of 30 prosperous nations, including smaller economies such as Taiwan and Israel, only Russia and Mexico have a greater maldistribution of income than the US.

"We choose to let the market determine most everything," says Timothy Smeeding, a public policy professor at the Maxwell School of Syracuse University, who compiled these inequality numbers. "We do far less on the social side. We have not as good a safety net. The priorities aren't there. Other countries make other choices."

Under Prime Minister Tony Blair, for example, Britain has made a costly and concerted effort to help its poorest families have a more equal chance for the education and other benefits that money can provide. Now, 5 percent of Britain's poor are better off than America's poor. Before 1995, none were.

In the US, both Republicans and Democrats voted several years ago to reform the welfare system — a change that Professor Smeeding generally approves. As a result, the number of those on welfare, often women with children, declined from 5 million in 1994 to 2.2 million in 2000.

But that reform "transformed the welfare poor into the working poor," he adds. They earn minimum wage, or just a bit better, and receive insufficient support from the government in the way of child care, earned income tax credits, cheap housing, and other assistance to rise out of poverty.

The US has the worst distribution of income of any well-to-do country.

That lack of government support makes them poorer than those in countries with stronger safety nets. At the request of the [*Christian Science*] *Monitor*, two of Smeeding's colleagues, Lee Rainwater and Markus Jantti, calculated the point at which residents of several other wealthy nations are better off in purchasing power than those similarly placed on the US income ladder. Besides the Canadian and Norwegian examples above, 12 percent of the poorest Finns, Swedes, and Dutch do better on average than the poorest 12 percent in the US; 15 percent of the German poor outdo 15 percent of the American poor; and 20 percent of Belgian poor beat the US poor.

Child Poverty in America

Smeeding also compared the poverty of American children (using the income of their families) with that of children in the world's 19 richest nations. He finds that the US stands among those with the highest child-poverty rates when the comparison is made on the basis of purchasing power. In most cases, foreign poor children are far better off.

The US stands among those with the highest child-poverty rates.

"Our low-income children are at a serious economic disadvantage compared to their counterparts in other nations," he concludes.

Of course, well-to-do American families, far ahead of most prosperous families in the other nations, can provide their children with all the benefits their good incomes can provide—nutritious food, computer courses, travel, expensive universities, etc. They get a degree, develop a good career, find a suitable educated marriage partner, and have probably one or two kids.

These advantages can put them well ahead in life—reinforcing what some observers see as a growing class structure in the US as the income distribution has worsened in recent decades.

But what about the poor children in America? Are they being left behind?

Whatever one thinks about income inequality, if the US doesn't do a better job in supporting the children of low-income families, says Smeeding, the nation faces "a rough future. They will be a drag on themselves and on our whole economy."

2

The Poor in the United States Live Comfortably

Robert E. Rector and Kirk A. Johnson

Robert E. Rector is a senior research fellow in Domestic Policy Studies at the Heritage Foundation, and Kirk A. Johnson is a senior policy analyst at the foundation's Center for Data Analysis.

In 2003, the Census Bureau's annual report claimed that there were 35 million poor persons in the United States. While most Americans believe the poor are hungry or living in poor housing, this is not the case. Today's poor live in conditions that would have been considered comfortable a few generations ago. For example, the average poor person has air conditioning, a microwave, two televisions, and a VCR or DVD player. Poor people typically own homes that are in good repair and provide adequate living space. Furthermore, the poor generally do not suffer from long-term hunger or malnutrition. While poor American families do sometimes face difficulties paying their bills on time, overall these families do not suffer hardship or deprivation.

Poverty is an important and emotional issue. Last year [2003], the Census Bureau released its annual report on poverty in the United States declaring that there were nearly 35 million poor persons living in this country in 2002, a small increase from the preceding year. To understand poverty in

America, it is important to look behind these numbers—to look at the actual living conditions of the individuals the government deems to be poor.

America's Poor Live Comfortably

For most Americans, the word "poverty" suggests destitution: an inability to provide a family with nutritious food, clothing, and reasonable shelter. But only a small number of the 35 million persons classified as "poor" by the Census Bureau fit that description. While real material hardship certainly does occur, it is limited in scope and severity. Most of America's "poor" live in material conditions that would be judged as comfortable or well-off just a few generations ago. Today, the expenditures per person of the lowest-income one-fifth (or quintile) of households equal those of the median American household in the early 1970s, after adjusting for inflation. . . .

As a group, America's poor are far from being chronically undernourished. The average consumption of protein, vitamins, and minerals is virtually the same for poor and middle-class children and, in most cases, is well above recommended norms. Poor children actually consume more meat than do higher-income children and have average protein intakes 100 percent above recommended levels. Most poor children today are, in fact, supernourished and grow up to be, on average, one inch taller and 10 pounds heavier that the GIs who stormed the beaches of Normandy in World War II.

While the poor are generally well-nourished, some poor families do experience hunger, meaning a temporary discomfort due to food shortages. According to the U.S. Department of Agriculture (USDA), 13 percent of poor families and 2.6 percent of poor children experience hunger at some point during the year. In most cases, their hunger is short-term. Eighty-nine percent of the poor report their families have "enough" food to eat, while only 2 percent say they "often" do not have enough to eat.

Overall, the typical American defined as poor by the government has a car, air conditioning, a refrigerator, a stove, a clothes washer and dryer, and a microwave. He has two color televisions, cable or satellite TV reception, a VCR or DVD player, and a stereo. He is able to obtain medical care. His home is in good repair and is not overcrowded. By his own report, his family is not hungry and he had sufficient funds in the past year to meet his family's essential needs. While this individual's life is not opulent, it is equally far from the popular images of dire poverty conveyed by the press, liberal activists, and politicians.

While [the typical poor American's] life is not opulent, it is equally far from ... popular images of dire poverty.

Of course, the living conditions of the average poor American should not be taken as representing all the poor. There is actually a wide range in living conditions among the poor. For example, over a quarter of poor households have cell phones and telephone answering machines, but, at the other extreme, approximately one-tenth have no phone at all. While the majority of poor households do not experience significant material problems, roughly a third do experience at least one problem such as overcrowding, temporary hunger, or difficulty getting medical care.

The best news is that remaining poverty can readily be reduced further, particularly among children. There are two main reasons that American children are poor: Their parents don't work much, and fathers are absent from the home.

In good economic times or bad, the typical poor family with children is supported by only 800 hours of work during a year: That amounts to 16 hours of work per week. If work in each family were raised to 2,000 hours per year—the equivalent of one adult working 40 hours per week throughout the year—nearly 75 percent of poor children would be lifted out of official poverty.

Father absence is another major cause of child poverty. Nearly two-thirds of poor children reside in single-parent homes; each year, an additional 1.3 million children are born out of wedlock. If poor mothers married the fathers of their children, almost three-quarters would immediately be lifted out of poverty. . . .

Housing

Some 46 percent of poor households own their own home. The typical home owned by the poor is a three-bedroom house with one-and-a-half baths. It has a garage or carport and a porch or patio and is located on a half-acre lot. The house was constructed in 1967 and is in good repair. The median value of homes owned by poor households was $86,600 in 2001 or 70 percent of the median value of all homes owned in the United States.

Some 73 percent of poor households own a car or truck; nearly a third own two or more cars or trucks. Over three-quarters have air conditioning; by contrast, 30 years ago, only 36 percent of the general U.S. population had air conditioning. Nearly three-quarters of poor households own microwaves; a third have automatic dishwashers.

Poor households are well-equipped with modern entertainment technology. It should come as no surprise that nearly all (97 percent) poor households have color TVs, but more than half actually own two or more color televisions. One-quarter own large-screen televisions, 78 percent have a VCR or DVD player, and almost two-thirds have cable or satellite TV reception. Some 58 percent own a stereo. More than a third have telephone answering machines, while a quarter have personal computers. While these numbers do not suggest lives of luxury, they are notably different from conventional images of poverty. . . .

Both the overall U.S. population and the poor in America live, in general, in very spacious housing. . . . [Seventy] percent of all U.S. households have two or more rooms per tenant. Among the poor, this figure is 68 percent.

Crowding is quite rare; only 2.5 percent of all households and 5.7 percent of poor households are crowded with more than one person per room. . . .

Housing space can also be measured by the number of square feet per person. The Residential Energy Consumption survey conducted by the U.S. Department of Energy shows that Americans have an average of 721 square feet of living space per person. Poor Americans have 439 square feet. Reasonably comparable international square-footage data are provided by the Housing Indicator Program of the United Nations Centre for Human Settlements, which surveyed housing conditions in major cities in 54 different nations. This survey showed the United States to have by far the most spacious housing units, with 50 percent to 100 percent more square footage per capita than city dwellers in other industrialized nations.

Poor households are well-equipped with modern entertainment technology.

America's poor compare favorably with the general population of other nations in square footage of living space. The average poor American has more square footage of living space than does the average person living in London, Paris, Vienna, and Munich. Poor Americans have nearly three times the living space of average urban citizens in middle-income countries such as Mexico and Turkey. Poor American households have seven times more housing space per person than the general urban population of very-low-income countries such as India and China. . . .

Housing Quality

Of course, it might be possible that the housing of poor American households could be spacious but still dilapidated or unsafe. However, data from the American Housing Survey indicate that such is not the case. For example, the survey provides a tally of households with "severe physical problems." Only a tiny portion of poor households and an even smaller portion of total households fall into that category.

The most common "severe problem," according to the American Housing Survey, is a shared bathroom, which occurs when occupants lack a bathroom and must share bathroom facilities with individuals in a neighboring unit. This condition affects about 1 percent of all U.S. households and 2 percent of all poor households. About one-half of 1 percent (0.5 percent) of all households and 2 percent of poor households have other "severe physical problems." The most common are repeated heating breakdowns and upkeep problems.

The average poor American has more . . . living space than does the average person living in London, Paris, Vienna, and Munich.

The American Housing Survey also provides a count of households affected by "moderate physical problems." A wider range of households falls into this category—9 percent of the poor and nearly 5 percent of total households. However, the problems affecting these units are clearly modest. While living in such units might be disagreeable by modern middle-class standards, they are a far cry from Dickensian squalor. The most common problems are upkeep, lack of a full kitchen, and use of unvented oil, kerosene or gas heaters as the primary heat source. (The last condition occurs almost exclusively in the South.)

Hunger and Malnutrition in America

There are frequent charges of widespread hunger and malnutrition in the United States. To understand these assertions, it is important, first of all, to distinguish between hunger and the more severe problem of malnutrition. Malnutrition (also called undernutrition) is a condition of reduced health due to a chronic shortage of calories and nutriments. There is little or no evidence of poverty-induced malnutrition in the United States.

Hunger is a far less severe condition: a temporary but real discomfort caused by an empty stomach. The government defines hunger as "the uneasy or painful sensation caused by lack of food." While hunger due to a lack of financial resources does occur in the United States, it is limited in scope and duration. According to the USDA, on a typical day, fewer than one American in 200 will experience hunger due to a lack of money to buy food. The hunger rate rises somewhat when examined over a longer time period; according to the USDA, some 6.9 million Americans, or 2.4 percent of the population, were hungry at least once during 2002. Nearly all hunger in the United States is short-term and episodic rather than continuous. . . .

Among the poor, the hunger rate was obviously higher: During 2002, 12.8 percent of the poor lived in households in which at least one member experienced hunger at some point. Among poor children, 2.4 percent experienced hunger at some point in the year. Overall, most poor households were not hungry and did not experience food shortages during the year.

When asked, some 89 percent of poor households reported they had "enough food to eat" during the entire year, although not always the kinds of food they would prefer. Around 9 percent stated they "sometimes" did not have enough to eat because of a lack of money to buy food. Another 2 percent of the poor stated that they "often" did not have enough to eat due to a lack of funds.

Nearly all hunger in the United States is short-term and episodic rather than continuous.

It is widely believed that a lack of financial resources forces poor people to eat low-quality diets that are deficient in nutriments and high in fat. However, survey data show that nutriment density (amount of vitamins, minerals, and protein per kilocalorie of food) does not vary by income class. Nor do the poor consume higher-fat diets than do the middle class; the percentage of persons with high fat intake (as a share of total calories) is virtually the same for low-income and upper-middle-income persons. Overconsumption of calories in general, however, is a major problem among the poor, as it is within the general U.S. population.

Age and gender play a far greater role than income class in determining nutritional intake.

Examination of the average nutriment consumption of Americans reveals that age and gender play a far greater role than income class in determining nutritional intake. For example, the nutriment intakes of adult women in the upper middle class (with incomes above 350 percent of the poverty level) more closely resemble the intakes of poor women than they do those of upper-middle-class men, children, or teens. The average nutriment consumption of upper-middle-income preschoolers, as a group, is virtually identical with that of poor preschoolers but not with the consumption of adults or older children in the upper middle class. . . .

Government surveys provide little evidence of widespread undernutrition among poor children; in fact, they show that the average nutriment consumption among the poor closely resembles that of the upper middle class. For example, children in families with incomes below the poverty level actually consume more meat than do children in families with incomes at 350 percent of the poverty level or higher (roughly $65,000 for a family of four in today's dollars). . . .

Poor Children's Weight and Stature

On average, poor children are very well-nourished, and there is no evidence of widespread significant undernutrition. For example, two indicators of undernutrition among the young are "thinness" (low weight for height) and stuntedness (low height for age). These problems are rare to nonexistent among poor American children.

The generally good health of poor American children can be illustrated by international comparisons. . . . Children are judged to be short or "stunted" if their height falls below the 2.3 percentile level of standard height-to-age table. . . .

In developing nations as a whole, some 43 percent of children are stunted. In Africa, more than a third of young children are affected; in Asia, nearly half. By contrast, in the United States, some 2.6 percent of young children in poor households are stunted by a comparable standard—a rate only slightly above the expected standard for healthy, well-nourished children. While concern for the well-being of poor American children is always prudent, the data overall underscore how large and well-nourished poor American children are by global standards.

Throughout this century, improvements in nutrition and health have led to increases in the rate of growth and ultimate height and weight of American children. Poor children have clearly benefited from this trend. Poor boys today at ages 18 and 19 are actually taller and heavier than boys of similar age in the general U.S. population in the late 1950s. Poor boys living today are one inch taller and some 10 pounds heavier than GIs of similar age during World War II, and nearly two inches taller and 20 pounds heavier than American doughboys back in World War I. . . .

Living Conditions and Hardships Among the Poor

Overall, the living standards of most poor Americans are far higher than is generally appreciated. The overwhelming majority of poor families are well-housed, have adequate food, and enjoy a wide range of modern amenities, including air conditioning and cable television. Some 70 percent of poor households report that during the course of the past year they were able to meet "all essential expenses," including mortgage, rent, utility bills, and important medical care.

However, two caveats should be applied to this generally optimistic picture. First, many poor families have difficulty paying their regular bills and must scramble to make ends meet. For example, around one-quarter of poor families are late in paying the rent or utility bills at some point during the year.

Poor boys today . . . are actually taller and heavier than boys of similar age . . . in the late 1950s.

Second, the living conditions of the average poor household should not be taken to represent all poor households. There is a wide range of living conditions among the poor; while more than a quarter of the poor have cell phones and answering machines, a tenth of the poor have no telephone at all. While most of America's poor live in accommodations with two or more rooms per person, roughly a tenth of the poor are crowded, with less than one room per person. . . .

During at least one month in the preceding year, some 20 percent of poor households reported they were unable to pay their fuel, gas, or electric bills promptly; around 4 percent had their utilities cut off at some point due to nonpayment. Another 13 percent of poor households failed, at some point in the year, to make their full monthly rent or mortgage payments, and 1 percent were evicted due to failure to pay rent. One in 10 poor families had their phones disconnected due to nonpayment at some time during the preceding year.

Some 70 percent of poor households . . . were able to meet 'all essential expenses.'

Overall, more than one-quarter of poor families experienced at least one financial difficulty during the year. Most had a late payment of rent or utility bills. Some 12 percent had phones or utilities cut off or were evicted. . . .

Some 14 percent lacked medical insurance and had a family member who needed to go to a doctor or hospital but did not go; 11 percent experienced hunger in the household; and around 9 percent were overcrowded, with more than one person per room. Slightly less than 4 percent of poor households experienced upkeep problems with the physical conditions of their apartments or homes. . . .

Overall Hardship

The most common problem facing poor households was late payment of rent or utilities. While having difficulty paying monthly bills is stressful, in most cases late payment did not result in material hardship or deprivation. . . . Some 22 percent had one problem, and 12 percent had two or more problems.

While it is appropriate to be concerned about the difficulties faced by some poor families, it is important to keep these problems in perspective. Many poor families have intermittent difficulty paying rent or utility bills but remain very well-housed by historic or international standards. Even poor families who are overcrowded and hungry, by U.S. standards, are still likely to have living conditions that are far above the world average.

3

Most Workers Do Not Suffer Long-Term Poverty

Thomas Sowell

Thomas Sowell has written Black Rednecks and White Liberals *and* The Quest for Cosmic Justice. *He is a senior fellow at the Hoover Institution at Stanford University.*

Very few Americans are truly "working poor." Most of the "working poor" are either part-time workers or young and inexperienced. Most people who start in the bottom 20 percent will move out of that group. Those that do not should not receive higher minimum wages because this will reduce the motivation for them to acquire new skills and make responsible decisions that will improve their working situations.

BusinessWeek magazine has joined the chorus of misleading rhetoric about "the working poor."

Why is this misleading? Let me count the ways.

First, Census data show that most people who are working are not poor and most people who are poor are not working.

The front-page headline on the May 31st [2004] issue of *BusinessWeek* says: "One in four workers earns $18,800 a year or less, with few if any benefits. What can be done?"

Only One-Twelfth of Workers

Buried inside is an admission that about a third of these are

Thomas Sowell, "Let's Discuss the 'Working Poor', Truth Would Be More Help than Welfare Statism," *Charleston Daily Mail,* June 3, 2004, p. 4.A. Copyright © 2004 by Charleston Newspapers. Reproduced by permission of the Creators Syndicate.

part-time workers and another third are no more than 25 years old.

So we are really talking about one-third of one fourth — or fewer than 10 percent of the workers — who are "working poor" in any full-time, long-run sense.

Nevertheless, the personal human interest stories and the photographs in the article are about people in this one-twelfth, even though the statistics are about the one-fourth.

As for "What can be done?" that is a misleading question. The article is about what other people can do for the "working poor," not what they can do for themselves, much less what they did in the past—or failed to do—that led to their having such low earning capacity.

The theme is that these are people trapped by external circumstances, and words like "moxie" and "gumption" are mentioned only sarcastically, to be dismissed along with "Horatio Alger."

But the cold fact is that what the intelligentsia call the American Dream is no dream.

An absolute majority of the people who were in the bottom 20 percent in income in 1975 have since then also been in the top 20 percent. This inconvenient fact has been out there for years—and has been ignored for years by those who want more government programs to relieve individuals from responsibility for making themselves more productive and therefore higher-income earners.

While the economy is "rewarding the growing ranks of educated knowledge workers," *BusinessWeek* says, this is not so for "workers who lack skills and training."

Business Should Not Create Entitlements

In a country with free education available through high school and heavily subsidized state colleges and universities, why do some people lack skills and training?

More important, what is likely to cause them to get skills and training—pay differentials or largess in money or in kind from the taxpayers as "entitlements"?

This is an agenda article, and facts that get in the way of the welfare state agenda get little attention, if any. Meanwhile, notions that have no factual basis are asserted boldly.

For example: "Working one's way up the ladder is becoming harder, not easier." Evidence? Wage rates for people in the bottom 20 percent have not risen much over the past 30 years.

The fallacy here is that it is not the same people in the bottom 20 percent over the past 30 years. Most people in the bottom 20 percent do not stay there even one decade, much less three. Young, inexperienced beginners do not remain young or inexperienced or beginners their whole lives.

Some people, of course, never learn—and never rise. Creating entitlements for them reduces any need to learn. But that is the way *BusinessWeek* urges us to go.

It wants higher minimum wages imposed, despite evidence that minimum-wage laws reduce employment. Why would anyone think that making labor more costly would not affect employment, when higher prices reduce the amount of anything else that is bought?

BusinessWeek wants "better day-care options"—"especially for single moms."

In other words, unmarried girls should have babies and expect the taxpayers to pick up the tab for taking care of them. And if we subsidize such irresponsible decisions, will that not have the same effects as subsidizing other things?

Most people in the bottom 20 percent do not stay there even one decade, much less three.

Another liberal notion promoted by *BusinessWeek* is making it "easier to form unions." Workers can get unionized right now just by voting for a union in a government-supervised election. How much easier should it be?

The problem is not a difficulty in forming unions.

What has happened is that workers themselves increasingly vote against unions because they have learned the hard way that unions cost jobs, even if *BusinessWeek* is unwilling to learn that lesson.

4

It Is Difficult for the Working Poor to Escape Poverty

David K. Shipler

David K. Shipler has written for The New York Times, *the* New Yorker, *the* Washington Post, *and the* Los Angeles Times. *He is the author of* Russia: Broken Idols, Solemn Dreams; Arab and Jew: Wounded Spirits in a Promised Land, *for which he won a Pulitzer Prize; and* The Working Poor: Invisible in America.

The poor often cannot make enough to pay their bills on time, even working full-time and receiving government subsidies. Available jobs frequently pay little and offer no hope for advancement. Any pay raise is often countered with a corresponding drop in government benefits. The constant struggle to stay afloat from day to day means there is nothing left over with which to obtain the additional training or education needed to escape poverty. Without higher paying jobs that will allow them to pursue greater education and training, the poor will stay poor.

Christie did a job that this labor-hungry economy could not do without. Every morning she drove her battered '86 Volkswagen from her apartment in public housing to the YWCA's child-care center in Akron, Ohio, where she spent the day watching over little children so their parents could go to work. Without her and thousands like her across the country, there would have been fewer people able to fill the jobs that fueled America's prosperity. Without her patience and warmth, children could have been harmed as well, for she was more than a baby-sitter. She gave the youngsters an emotionally safe place, taught and mothered them, and sometimes even rescued them from abuse at home.

For those valuable services, she received a check for about $330 every two weeks. She could not afford to put her own two children in the day-care center where she worked.

[Christie] could not afford to put her own two children in the day-care center where she worked.

Christie was a hefty woman who laughed more readily than her predicament should have allowed. She suffered from stress and high blood pressure. She had no bank account because she could not keep enough money long enough. Try as she might to shop carefully, she always fell behind on her bills and was peppered with late fees. Her low income entitled her to food stamps and a rental subsidy, but whenever she got a little pay raise, government agencies reduced the benefits, and she felt punished for working. She was trapped on the treadmill of welfare reform, running her life according to the rules of the Personal Responsibility and Work Opportunity Reconciliation Act of 1996. The title left no doubt about what Congress and the White House saw as poverty's cause and solution.

The Personal Responsibility and Work Opportunity Reconciliation Act

Initially the new law combined with the good economy to send welfare caseloads plummeting. As states were granted flexibility in administering time limits and work requirements, some created innovative consortiums of government, industry, and charity to guide people into effective job training and employment. But most available jobs had three unhappy traits:

They paid low wages, offered no benefits, and led nowhere. "Many who do find jobs," the Urban Institute concluded in a 2002 report, "lose other supports designed to help them, such as food stamps and health insurance, leaving them no better off—and sometimes worse off—than when they were not working."

Christie considered herself such a case. The only thing in her wallet resembling a credit card was a blue-green piece of plastic labeled "Ohio" and decorated with a drawing of a lighthouse projecting a beam into the night. Inside the "O" was a gold square—a computer chip. On the second working day of every month, she slipped the card into a special machine at Walgreen's, Save-A-Lot, or Apple's, and punched in her identification number. A credit of $136 was loaded into her chip. This was the form in which her "food stamps" were now issued—less easy to steal or to sell, and less obvious and degrading in the checkout line.

Most available jobs had three unhappy traits: They paid low wages, offered no benefits, and led nowhere.

The card contained her first bit of income in every month and permitted her first expenditure. It could be used for food only, and not for cooked food or pet food. It occupied the top line in the balance sheet she kept for me during a typical October.

"2nd Spent 136.00 food stamps," she wrote. So the benefit was all gone the day she got it. Three days later she had to come up with an additional $25 in cash for groceries, another $54 on October 10, and $15 more on the twelfth. Poor families typically find that food stamps cover only one-half to three-quarters of their grocery costs.

Struggling with the System

Even the opening balance on the card was chipped away as Christie inched up in salary. It makes sense that the benefit is based on income: the less you need, the less you get. That's the economic side. On the psychological side, however, it produces hellish experiences for the beneficiaries. Every three months Christie had to take half a day off from work (losing half a day's wages) and carry an envelope full of pay stubs, utility bills, and rent receipts to be pawed over by her ill-tempered caseworker, who applied a state-mandated formula to figure her food stamp allotment and her children's eligibility for health insurance. When Christie completed a training course and earned a raise of 10 cents an hour, her food stamps dropped by $10 a month.

Many former welfare recipients ... would rather forfeit their rights than contend with the hassle and humiliation.

That left her $6 a month ahead, which was not nothing but felt like it. Many former welfare recipients who go to work just say good riddance to the bureaucracies that would provide food stamps, medical coverage, and housing. Some think wrongly that they're no longer eligible once they're off welfare; others would rather forfeit their rights than contend with the hassle and humiliation. Quiet surrender ran against Christie's grain, however. She was smart and insistent, as anyone must be to negotiate her way through the system. She never flinched from appealing to higher authority. When she once forgot to put a utilities bill in her sheaf of papers, her caseworker withheld her food stamps. "I mailed it to her the next day," Christie said. Two weeks passed, and the card remained empty. Christie called the caseworker. "She got really snotty," Christie remembered. "'Well, didn't I tell you you were supposed to send some documentation?'"

"I was like, 'Have you checked your mail?'" No, as it turned out, the caseworker's mail had piled up unread. "She was like, 'Well, I got people waiting up to two, three months on food stamps.' And she didn't get back with me. I had to go to her supervisor." The benefits were then restored.

It is easy to lose your balance having one foot planted tentatively in the working world and the other still entwined in this thicket of red tape. Managing relations with a boss, finding reliable child care, and coping with a tangle of unpaid bills can be daunting enough for a single mother with little such experience; add surveillance by a bureaucracy that seems more prosecutor than provider, and you have Christie's high blood pressure.

While she invoked the system's rules to get her due, she also cheated—or thought she did. Living with her surreptitiously was her boyfriend, Kevin, the father of her son. She was certain that if the Housing Authority knew, she would be evicted, either because he was a convicted felon (two years for assault) or because his earning power, meager though it was, would have lifted her beyond eligibility. So slight are the margins between government assistance and outright destitution that small lies take on large significance in the search for survival.

Kevin looked like a friendly genie—a solid 280 pounds, a shaved head, and a small earring in his right ear. His income was erratic. In decent weather he made $7.40 an hour working for a landscaper, who rewarded him with a free turkey to end the season at Thanksgiving—and then dumped him onto unemployment for the winter. He wanted to drive a truck or cut meat. He had received a butcher's certificate in a training course during imprisonment, but when he showed the document from the penitentiary, employers didn't rush to put a knife in his hand.

Paying the Bills

The arithmetic of Christie's life added up to tension, and you had to look hard through her list of expenditures to find fun or luxury. On the fifth she received her weekly child support check of $37.68 from Kevin (she got nothing from her daughter's father, who was serving a long prison sentence for assault). The same day, she put $5 worth of gas in her car, and the next day spent $6 of her own money to take the day-care kids to the zoo. The eighth was payday, and her entire $330 check disappeared in a flash. First, there was what she called a $3 "tax" to cash her check, just one of several such fees for money orders and the like—a penalty for having no checking account. Immediately, $172 went for rent, including a $10 late fee, which she was always charged because she never had enough to pay by the first of the month. Then, because it was October and she had started to plan for Christmas, she paid $31.47 at a store for presents she had put on layaway, another $10 for gasoline, $40 to buy shoes for her two kids, $5 for a pair of corduroy pants at a secondhand shop, another $5 for a shirt, $10 for bell-bottom pants, and $47 biweekly for car insurance. The $330 was gone. She had no insurance on her TVs, clothes, furniture, or other household goods.

It is easy to lose your balance having one foot planted tentatively in the working world and the other still entwined in this thicket of red tape.

Utilities and other bills got paid out of her second check toward the end of the month. Her phone usually cost about $43 a month, gas for the apartment $34, electricity $46, and prescriptions between $8 and $15. Her monthly car payment ran $150, medical insurance $72, and cable TV $43. Cable is no longer considered a luxury by low-income families that pinch and sacrifice to have it. So much of modern American culture now comes through television that the poor would be further marginalized without the broad access that cable provides. Besides, it's relatively cheap entertainment. "I just have basic," Christie explained. "I have an antenna, but you can't see anything, you get no reception." And she needed good reception because she and Kevin loved to watch wrestling.

Food

One reason for Christie's tight budget was the abundance of high-priced, well-advertised snacks, junk food, and prepared meals that provide an easy fallback diet for a busy working mother—or for anyone who has never learned to cook from scratch. Besides the staples of hamburger and chicken, "I buy sausages," Christie said, "I buy the TV dinners 'cause I might be tired some days and throw it in the oven—like Salisbury steaks and turkey and stuff like that. My kids love pizza. I get the frozen pizzas. . . . I buy my kids a lot of breakfast things 'cause we're up early and we're out the door. You know, those cereal bars and stuff like that, they're expensive! You know? Pop Tarts, cereal bars, Granola." The cheaper breakfasts, like hot cereal, came only on weekends, when she had time. "They eat the hot cereal, but during the week we're on the go. So I give them cereal in the bag. My son likes to eat dry cereal, so I put him some cereal in the lunch bag. Cocoa Puffs. They got Cocoa Dots." She laughed. "Lucky Charms. He's not picky. My daughter's picky." Those candylike cereals soak up dollars. At my local supermarket, Lucky Charms cost dearly: $4.39 for a box of just 14 ounces, while three times as much oatmeal goes for nearly the same price, $4.29.

Recreation

Recreation for Christie and Kevin centered on food and drink. When her eleven-year-old daughter brought home a good report card, they rewarded her by scraping together a little cash for an evening at a modest restaurant, either Mexican or, if it was Wednesday, at Ryan's down the street. Wednesday was steak night at Ryan's, a big, boisterous, all-you-can-eat family place at the edge of the black neighborhood where they lived. The buffet counters, heaped with steaming potatoes and green beans and slabs of beef, were encircled by a jovial, multiracial crowd of grandparents, parents, and kids jostling one another with friendly apologies as they carried away piles of stick-to-your-ribs food for just nine bucks apiece.

As an occasional present to themselves, Christie and Kevin invited friends over, lit a charcoal fire in the metal barrel that had been made into a grill behind her ground-floor apartment, and feasted on barbecued chicken and ribs and lots of cans of Miller's. Did they drink to get drunk?

"Mmmmmmmm," Kevin replied in a long, low hum.

"Mmmmm," said Christie. "Not around my children. I go to the club for that. Then I come home and go to sleep." She gave a delighted laugh. She liked Boone's Farm wine, Manischewitz Cream, and Paul Masson brandy, which explained the entry in the records she kept for me: "15.00 on bottle" on October 12. But she was no alcoholic, and she and Kevin swore that they had stayed away from drugs despite the constant temptation in a neighborhood crawling with pushers.

It was strange that she thought of herself as lazy, because her work was exhausting.

"Christie likes to have fun," her mother said tartly. Her mother, "Gladys," had dropped out of high school, spent years on welfare, and nurtured the fervent dream of seeing her three children in college. The ambition propelled two of them. Christie's brother became an accountant, and her sister, a loan officer. But Christie never took to higher education. She began reluctantly at the University of Akron, lived at home, and finally got fed up with having no money. The second semester of her sophomore year, she went to work instead of to school, a choice that struck her then as less momentous than it turned out to be.

"She didn't take things as serious as they really were," Gladys complained. "Now she sees for herself how serious this is."

Just how serious depended on what she wanted to do. She loved working with children but now discovered that without a college degree she would have trouble getting hired at a responsible level in the Head Start preschool program, much less as a teacher in a regular school; she was limited to a YWCA day-care center whose finances were precarious. Since 95 percent of the Y's children came from low-income families, the fees were essentially set by the center's main source of income, Ohio's Department of Human Services, which paid $99 to $114 a week for full-time care. Given the center's heavy expenses, the rates were not enough to pay teachers more than $5.30 to $5.90 an hour.

Lazy?

Christie's previous jobs had also imprisoned her close to the minimum wage as a hostess-cashier at a Holiday Inn, a cashier at Kmart, a waitress in a bar, a cook and waitress and cashier in various restaurants. She had become a veteran of inadequate training programs designed to turn her into a retail salesperson, a bus driver, and a correctional officer, but the courses never enabled her and her classmates to pass the tests and get hired. She had two words to explain why she had never returned to college. "Lazy. Lazy."

It was strange that she thought of herself as lazy, because her work was exhausting, and her low wage required enormous effort to stay afloat. When the bills would inundate her, she explained, "I pay that one one month and don't pay that one and play catch-up on this one, one month. I play catch-up pretty much. I rotate 'em around. You got a phone bill. You got to pay that every month. If you miss a payment, pssshhh. It's double the next month and triple the next month. The next thing, you got a disconnect. I live on disconnect notices. And I pay my bill every month, but get a disconnect every month, because everybody wants you to pay on the first of the month. I don't get paid on the first of the month. I can't pay ten people on the first of the month. I get the disconnect notice, and I get very, very close. I call, I make payment arrangements. I'm like, 'Hey, please give me a break. Don't turn me off yet. I'm gonna send ya something,' you know. The car dealer man, I might not take him all of my 150, but I take him something. They're funny guys. They work with me, they're real nice. And he said, 'Well, Miss V, what do you have for us today?' One thing the guy said, he said, 'I notice you come every month with something.' And I do. I come with the majority. Every month. I'm like, 'Hey, I gotta buy food, fellas.'"

In her life, every small error had large consequences.

Her strained schedule made her vulnerable to fees and fines, including one that ended her children's summer day care. Because she couldn't afford the $104 a month it would have cost to put her kids part-time in the Y's day-care center, her mother watched them after school. In the summer they went to a Boys and Girls Club for a token $7 each. But the club had a strict rule about pickup times—3 p.m. except Friday, when it was 1. One Friday, her mother forgot the earlier deadline. Instead of calling Christie at work, the club started the clock running, imposing a fine that began at $10 apiece for the first five minutes and continued at a lower rate until her mother finally appeared, more than an hour late. It reached $80 per child, an impossible amount for Christie to afford, so her children could not continue. In her life, every small error had large consequences.

Trapped in Low-Paying Jobs

Christie seemed doomed to a career of low pay without the chance of significant promotion, no matter how important her jobs might be to the country's well-being. At her level in the economy, everything would have to be perfectly aligned to open the door to comfort. After the missteps at the outset of her adulthood, she would now need the boost of higher education or the right niche of vocational training. By itself, hard work alone would not pay off. That lesson, tainting such a revered virtue, is not one that we want to learn. But unless employers can and will pay a good deal more for the society's essential labor, those working hard at the edge of poverty will stay there. And America's rapturous hymn to work will sound a sour note.

5

The Poor Often Lack Access to Health Care

James Mullahy and Barbara L. Wolfe

James Mullahy is a professor of preventive medicine. Barbara L. Wolfe is a professor of economics and preventive medicine. They both teach at the University of Wisconsin–Madison.

By any measure, the poor are less healthy than those who are not poor. Poor children are not as healthy as other children, for example, and the poor have a greater risk of mental disorders. Yet despite their greater need for health care, the poor have less access to health care and the care they do receive is of inferior quality. They also have a harder time finding affordable health care because many low-wage workers are not covered by private insurance and the majority of people are not covered by Medicaid. Even those who are enrolled in Medicaid may face problems getting care because some providers refuse Medicaid patients. The result is that the poor are less likely to receive preventive medical care or see a doctor even for serious health problems.

Health in the United States is very strongly correlated with income. Poor people are less healthy than those who are better off, whether our benchmark is mortality, the numbers with acute or chronic diseases and impairments, or people's own assessment of their health. In this article, we explore the

James Mullahy and Barbara L. Wolfe, "Health Policies for the Nonelderly Poor," *Focus,* vol. 21, number 2, Fall 2000, pp. 32–36. Reproduced by permission.

relationship between health and poverty and examine some of the difficulties facing low-income Americans in gaining access to health care.

Health and the Poverty Population

Compared to those who are not poor, the health of the poor is more exposed to risk, whether unintentional (lead paint poisoning) or voluntary (use of tobacco). When poor people become sick, they have less access to health care and the quality of the care that they do obtain appears to be inferior. One major indicator of the link between income and poverty is a significantly greater premature mortality from many causes among the poor. . . . Being poor *and* living in poorer neighborhoods appear to be associated with generally worse health and earlier death.

In the prosperous decade of the 1990s, those who were not poor became healthier; disconcertingly, the poor and the near-poor saw little or no improvement in their health. Children's health provides telling evidence of this growing inequality. The health of nonpoor children has improved considerably over the past few decades, that of poor children hardly at all. One salient example is lead poisoning. Lead, often present in lead-laden paint and dust in older houses, puts children at risk of impaired intelligence, learning disabilities, hyperactivity, and other behavioral problems. In 1988–91, 16 percent of young children in low-income families—but only 4 percent in higher-income families—had levels of lead in the blood high enough to do damage. A report based on survey data from 1988 through 1994 found that over 8 percent of children on Medicaid still had high lead levels—this after two or more decades of effort to reduce lead poisoning.

There is also a clear correlation between mental health and poverty. Those on the lowest rungs of the socioeconomic ladder are 2.5 times more likely to suffer from mental disorders than those in the highest socioeconomic group. Children in families characterized by multigenerational poverty manifest a high rate of mental illness.

The health of nonpoor children has improved considerably over the past few decades, that of poor children hardly at all.

Other risk factors, such as homelessness or minority status, compound the effect of poverty. The poorest of the poor—homeless adults—are mostly uninsured and disproportionately in poor health. One-quarter to a third have severe mental illness, about half have a history of alcohol abuse, and about a third of drug abuse. Homelessness itself can lead to malnutrition and exposure to infectious disease. Being homeless hinders treatment for illness: continuing contact with medical providers and adherence to complex treatment regimes is very difficult for homeless people, and living in shelters and on the streets is hardly conducive to recuperation.

African Americans, who are disproportionately poor, are also disproportionately subject to high blood pressure, coronary heart disease, diabetes and its complications, and sudden infant death syndrome. The higher rate of teen out-of-wedlock births among African Americans and Hispanics increases the risk of infant mortality and low birth weight, and may produce a continuing relationship between poverty and poor health.

A major difficulty in understanding the relationship between health and poverty is determining what is cause and what is effect. For example, poor health may cause poverty by restricting the hours one can work and the kind of work one can do and by requiring costly medical care and services. But poverty may affect health by limiting one's ability to buy health insurance and to pay the direct and indirect costs of medical care. Poverty results in substandard housing or poor living conditions that may lead to ill health. But it is also possible that other, unobserved factors may drive both poverty and ill health: individuals who give little heed to the future may invest relatively little in education or other components of human capital *and* act in ways that put their health at risk.

Whatever the causes, the poor have a greater need of medical care than other groups. Yet in the United States, they very often find no ready access to care that they can afford. . . .

Private Insurance Coverage

About three-quarters of the population are covered by private plans, two-thirds of them through plans offered by employers. The tax system encourages this arrangement, because the contribution of employers to health insurance is not counted as part of an employee's taxable income. The value of this subsidy is not small ($86.4 billion in 2000, according to the U.S. Treasury). Because employer contributions represent a percentage of earnings, the subsidy is not evenly distributed, and it is worth much less to low-wage workers than to high-wage workers. Despite the subsidies, moreover, the cost of health care plans to businesses is high and growing, and more of it is being passed on to employees.

Poverty results in substandard housing or poor living conditions that may lead to ill health.

Among the employed, low-wage workers are much less likely to be offered private health insurance through their employers than are high-wage workers. The reason lies largely in the interactions between the costs of employer-provided health insurance and the tax subsidy of employer contributions. Employers who offer health insurance to employees do so by reducing cash compensation. They thus may not be able to shift all of the cost of health insurance to low-wage workers, especially those at or near the minimum wage. They may simply drop the health insurance plan or may offer insurance at so high a price that the employee declines coverage. With the possible exception of the last two years of a very tight labor market, since the late 1970s there has been a steady drop in the proportion of private-sector workers with employer-sponsored coverage, especially among the lowest-paid workers, whose coverage rates dropped by nearly 25 percent between 1987 and 1996.

Public Programs

Medicaid is the main public program providing health care coverage to low-income people. A joint federal-state program, it covers nearly 11 percent of the population. In 1997, 36 million low-income persons were enrolled, including slightly more than 18 percent of all children and about 60 percent of poor children. Total Medicaid expenditures were $160 billion.

Medicaid does not cover the majority of poor and near-poor adults and children, although eligibility has been steadily expanded in the last decade or so. Moreover, since the 1996 welfare reforms decoupled eligibility for Medicaid from welfare receipt, the number actually enrolled has been declining. Medicaid now requires a separate application, and access is tied to state eligibility levels from before 1996. The cutoff for eligibility is typically below the earnings from full-time, minimum-wage jobs. Former welfare recipients entering the workforce may thus lose public medical insurance for their children without being able to acquire private insurance.

Access to Medicaid is not particularly straightforward. First, eligibility can differ within families, so that an infant in a family may be eligible while older children are not. Second, Medicaid is all or nothing. Most low-income persons are either eligible or they are not. If their income rises by one dollar, they may lose all eligibility. Third, eligibility requirements and coverage vary from state to state. A poor single mother whose income is 75 percent of the poverty line may receive no coverage in one state, full coverage with few constraints in a second state, and limited coverage and difficulty finding a provider in a third state.

Medicaid does not cover the majority of poor and near-poor adults and children.

Problems of access continue even for those enrolled. Because of low reimbursement rates, providers in some states refuse Medicaid patients. Urban areas with heavy concentrations of poor people and rural areas in general have difficulty attracting physicians. Hospital consolidations and shortages of other medical personnel compound these difficulties. Medicaid recipients may find their coverage limited to specific providers or health maintenance organizations that may not have clinics easily accessible to public transport or open when adults are not working. There may be long delays for an appointment, or long waits at the time of the appointment.

In essence, the current medical welfare system, incorporating Medicaid, general assistance, other public service delivery programs, and charity care, functions as a substitute for private health insurance. Consumers face an "either-or" choice: either rely completely on public medical programs or rely completely on privately purchased insurance and care. There are relatively weak incentives for low-income consumers to contribute partially toward the cost of their coverage, and for many, the additional benefit from private health insurance is less than its cost, given the existence of the public system. Thus the availability of the public system is an incentive to employees not to accept more expensive employer-offered insurance and an incentive to employers not to offer it. The size of this effect (known as "crowd-out") is unclear, but most estimates suggest that some of those people newly covered under public programs had or could have private, employer-based coverage.

Who Does Not Have Health Insurance?

In 1998, 16.3 percent of the entire U.S. population had no health insurance, public or private. For poor people, the problem was more severe: about a third of all poor, and between 40 and 50 percent of poor adults aged 18–44, had no health insurance for the entire year. Ethnic and racial minorities were twice or three times as likely to be uninsured as were non-Hispanic whites. Perhaps another 20 million people had too little health insurance to protect them from the financial burdens of a major illness.

Among those with poverty-level or near-poverty incomes, the percentage with private or public insurance was stagnant or falling from the mid-1980s until 1998. For many among the poor, being uninsured is not a transient but a long-term phenomenon. Over the three years 1993–96, 9.3 percent of the poor and 10 percent of the near-poor were without health insurance, compared to less than 1 percent of those with incomes four or more times the poverty line.

How Much Does Health Insurance Matter?

The amount and quality of health care that people use is influenced by many factors other than insurance. Income directly constrains choices about whether to seek care, the expense and time involved in getting to providers, and neighborhood environmental risks. Income also plays a critical indirect role, for example, in the extent of people's knowledge of appropriate medical care, of preventive measures, and of risk factors such as diet, exercise, smoking, and alcohol use. We should not expect that providing insurance will equalize the use of medical care or health status itself across all income groups. But would insurance coverage for all low-income persons influence their health and their use of medical care?

Certainly the *absence* of insurance has serious effects, especially when compounded by poverty. . . . The poorer the child, the greater the probability that he or she will not see a doctor.

For every income group, insured children are much more likely to see a doctor than uninsured children. But the difference between the insured and uninsured children is greater among the poor than among the other groups. The increase, between 1993–94 and 1995–96, in the proportion of uninsured near-poor and nonpoor children who had no physician contact suggests greater difficulty in obtaining care, perhaps due to the increase in managed care.

The poor receive less preventive medical care. Poor children aged 19–35 months are less likely to be vaccinated for measles than nonpoor children (86 versus 92 percent). In 1994, only 44 percent of low-income women over 40 had had a mammogram in the last two years, compared to 65 percent of nonpoor women. Epidemiological studies found that uninsured patients had a 25 percent higher risk of mortality than the privately insured.

The poorer the child, the greater the probability that he or she will not see a doctor.

The reasons for some of these problems are complex, and do not rest only with insurance but also with impediments arising from work schedules and household difficulties; some are certainly due to cultural and language impediments, others to forms of provider discrimination. But in general, the poor and uninsured are less likely to have a regular source of care, more likely to use emergency rooms to treat illnesses that are not life-threatening, more likely to be admitted to hospital for treatment of conditions such as asthma, hypertension, or diabetes that could have received outpatient treatment at an earlier point. There is evidence that uninsured persons with serious illnesses see doctors only half as often as the insured. In addition to delayed and forgone medical care, lack of coverage leads to financial insecurity for families, inequitable community burdens, and increased costs for businesses as the cost of caring for the uninsured is shifted to the insured.

More positively, the expansion of Medicaid insurance has reduced infant mortality rates, especially among African Americans. Access to health care information and services, mostly conveyed in clinical settings, is likely to be an important determinant of individual health—for example, reducing smoking and problem drinking, encouraging regular exercise and proper diet, providing prenatal information and care, or simple screening for hypertension.

For some years now, the relationship between poverty and health has been the focus of policymakers. The federal Department of Health and Human Services recently stated two central goals for the nation. The first—increasing the quality and years of healthy life—applies to all citizens. The second— eliminating health disparities—speaks directly to the problem we have described here: the effect of poverty on health status and on access to health care.

6

The Poor Do Not Lack Access to Health Care

Conrad F. Meier

Before his death in 2005, Conrad F. Meier worked for the Heartland Institute. He was the founding editor of Health Care News *and a Heartland senior fellow.*

While the U.S. Census Bureau claims that there are 44.9 million Americans without health insurance, this is incorrect. Fifteen million of these Americans qualify for Medicaid or State Children's Health Insurance Program. Instead of being considered as uninsured, these people should be considered as insured but not yet "activated." Moreover, many people who are in fact covered by Medicaid report being uninsured because they do not consider Medicaid to be health insurance. In addition, about 9 million more people counted as uninsured are not enrolled in health insurance because they are immigrants. Since the census data is therefore skewed, it should not be relied upon as a basis for formulating public policy.

New Census data ... reveal 243.3 million Americans were covered by health insurance in 2003, up 1 million from the previous year's figures. The number of people with health insurance has increased steadily for the past 15 years: The U.S. has never seen more people covered by insurance than it did in 2003.

At the same time, the Census Bureau reports 44.9 million Americans were without health insurance for some period of time during 2003. The uninsured, according to the Census Bureau, represented 15.6 percent of the U.S. population in 2003—no different from 1996.

15 Million Error

Census Bureau officials acknowledge their uninsured number is inflated, since Census data count as "uninsured" adults and children who are eligible for, but not enrolled in, Medicaid and the State Children's Health Insurance Program (S-CHIP).

According to Census data, more than 15 million "uninsured" individuals reside in households with annual incomes of less than $25,000. Most meet the income test for Medicaid or S-CHIP eligibility, but they are not enrolled.

When a person who is eligible for Medicaid but not enrolled in the program enters the health care system—through a hospital emergency room or outpatient clinic, for example—that person is automatically enrolled in the Medicaid plan. By definition, then, many—perhaps most—of these 15 million "uninsured" persons are folks who have not sought health care. Counting this population as "uninsured" gravely distorts the accuracy of the data, as these are individuals who can become insured at any time.

Frankly, there is no such thing as an "uninsured" individual eligible for Medicaid. For all intents and purposes, these Medicaid-eligibles should be considered *insured* persons who simply have not yet "activated" their insurance by seeking health care.

While employed as an analyst with the Center for Advanced Social Research at the University of Missouri-Columbia, I conducted research that found many Medicaid recipients say they don't have insurance coverage. When interviewed by a trained researcher and asked if the government pays for their medical care, they say yes. When asked if they remember the name of the government program, they cite Medicaid.

Many—perhaps most—of these 15 million 'uninsured' persons are folks who have not sought health care.

But many interviewees said they don't consider government-run health care to be insurance. This is not surprising, given that Medicaid recipients pay no premiums and often pay no deductibles or copayments for services they receive. So the Census Bureau data on the uninsured are skewed even more, since they include persons enrolled in Medicaid who report themselves to be uninsured.

Further skewing the Census Bureau's uninsured statistic is a sizeable increase in the immigrant population. Roughly 9 million documented and undocumented aliens are generally included in Census estimates. Many immigrants hesitate to participate in a government program of any kind for fear of establishing a paper trail for immigration and national security authorities. Cultural mores, folkways, and language barriers also conspire to keep these people uninsured.

Sending the Wrong Message

The Census Bureau says its data collection methodology "is not designed primarily to collect health insurance data." Yet it releases its new data with great fanfare, encouraging the data's misuse by politicians and other proponents of government interference in the health care marketplace.

The Census Bureau's inflated uninsured numbers send the wrong message to politicians. One of [2004] presidential candidate John Kerry's health care proposals single[d] out the Medicaid population for special legislation. His campaign literature note[d] there are "millions of uninsured children who are eligible for health care coverage under Medicaid or S-CHIP but are not enrolled." Spending millions of dollars to enroll these essentially insured Americans would make no difference in their access to health care, but would surely waste scarce tax dollars.

Many Medicaid recipients say they don't have [health] insurance.

Until the Census Bureau significantly revises its data collection and reporting methods, policymakers and the general public must not rely on these figures for making public policy. These data are known and acknowledged to be flawed; legislators and special interest advocates have no excuse for relying on these numbers when crafting public policy. This issue is too important for millions of dollars to be wasted on solutions built on wrong information.

7

Poverty Causes Terrorism

Quan Li and Drew Schaub

Quan Li and Drew Schaub are professors of political science at Pennsylvania State University.

A primary cause of terrorism is poverty. Because poverty causes feelings of military and economic inferiority, people affected by it choose violent means to express their discontent. Globalization and economic development, which helps to fight poverty, is linked to a decrease in terrorism. As a country's trade expands, foreign interests within the country become less-appealing targets for terrorists. Moreover, terrorists will be less likely to travel to economic partner countries to commit terrorist acts.

Advocates of the negative relationship between economic globalization and terrorism [i.e., that economic globalization reduces terrorism] claim that economic globalization removes an important cause of transnational terrorism. The emergence of this argument is quite recent, mostly as an immediate reaction to the terrorist events of September 11 [2001]. It is not surprising that the argument is not as well developed as those on the positive effect of globalization [i.e., that globalization increases terrorism] nor has it received as much attention from students of transnational terrorism. Economic globalization is argued to reduce transnational terrorist

Quan Li and Drew Schaub, "Economic Globalization and Transnational Terrorism: A Pooled Time-Series Analysis," *Journal of Conflict Resolution,* vol. 48, April 2004, pp. 236–39. Copyright © 2004 by Sage Publications. Reproduced by permission.

incidents because it facilitates economic development, which in turn removes an incentive to engage in terrorism.

The Causes of Transnational Terrorism

A primary cause of transnational terrorism is underdevelopment and poverty, an argument that recently became popular among but was rarely formalized by policy makers and scholars. Poor economic conditions create "terrorist breeding grounds," where disaffected populations turn to transnational terrorist activities as a solution to their problems. In [Palestinian writer] Marwan Bishara's words, "When people feel so inferior militarily and economically, they adopt asymmetric means—not the usual means—to get what they want." In addition, poverty, underdevelopment, and instability are often associated with those states either willing to provide safe haven for terrorists or unable to successfully expel terrorists from their borders. Poverty and its accompanying instability in Afghanistan created the conditions that allowed the Taliban to gain power, a situation that in turn led to the provision of sanctuary for Al Qaeda and Osama bin Laden. Consistent with this argument, [President George W.] Bush claims in a widely cited speech, "We fight against poverty because hope is an answer to terror."

Poverty and its accompanying instability in Afghanistan created the conditions that allowed the Taliban to gain power.

Recently, [economist Alan B.] Krueger and [professor Jitka] Maleckova assessed empirically the link between poverty or low education and participation in politically motivated violence and terrorist activities. They show that the occurrences of hate crimes, which resemble terrorism in spirit, are largely unrelated to economic conditions. Then, based on a public opinion poll conducted in the West Bank and Gaza Strip, they show that Palestinians who have higher education or living standards are just as likely to support violence against Israeli targets. Next, they conducted a statistical analysis of participation in [terrorist group] Hezbollah in Lebanon and found that education and poverty do not explain whether individuals choose to become martyrs for Hezbollah on suicide missions. Those who have a living standard above the poverty line or a secondary school or higher education are actually more likely to participate in Hezbollah. They also found that Israeli Jews involved in terrorist activities in the early 1980s were well educated and with well-paying jobs. Finally, they show that there is mixed evidence on the effect of real gross domestic product (GDP) growth on the number of terrorist acts each year from 1969 to 1996 in Israel. Krueger and Maleckova conclude that economic conditions and education are largely unrelated to individual participation in and support for terrorism.

Although interesting and innovative, the study by Krueger and Maleckova needs to be put into perspective. First, most of their cases come from a region that is characterized by historical tension, hatred, and military violence. Their conclusion may not generalize across all countries. Second, the positive relationship between a Hezbollah suicide bomber's education and suicide missions may merely reflect that terrorist leaders use education as a screening device to pick the most competent candidate possible. Without controlling for the job opportunities of the suicide bombers, Krueger and Maleckova are not directly testing their hypothesis. Third, the lack of correlation between poor economic conditions and terrorist activities at the individual level may not be inferred to hold at the country level. Better-educated people, living under good conditions in the poor countries, are also better informed about conditions in other rich countries than their poor countrymen and hence are more conscious of the comparison between the rich and their own countries. The sense of relative deprivation can provide a strong incentive for them to engage in terrorist activities as the last resort to change the conditions of their own countries. Their individual behaviors can lead one to observe at the aggregate level more terrorist incidents in the poor countries. Hence, we concur with Krueger and Maleckova that whether economic development is related to transnational terrorism at the country level should be assessed in cross-country analyses.

How Economic Globalization Fights Poverty and Terrorism

For economic globalization to reduce transnational terrorism, globalization has to be able to promote economic development and reduce poverty. Many policy makers have endorsed the positive effect of globalization on development. Canadian Finance Minister Paul Martin argues that participation in the global economic system greatly enhances a state's economic development. President Bush also says, "The vast majority of financing for development comes not from aid, but from trade and domestic capital and foreign investment. . . . So, to be serious about fighting poverty, we must be serious about expanding trade." U.S. Federal Reserve Board Chairman Alan Greenspan also claims that "the extraordinary changes in global finance on balance have been beneficial in facilitating significant improvements in economic structures and living standards throughout the world." Leaders of the seven major industrial democracies [known as the G7 nations] assert in the joint communiqué for the 1996 G7 Summit that "economic growth and progress in today's interdependent world is bound up with the process of globalization".

Scholars, however, have relatively more diverse opinions about the effect of economic globalization on development. On one hand, trade was considered to hinder growth in the developing countries in the 1950s. More recently, [economist Dani] Rodrik, has raised doubt about the positive effect of trade openness on economic growth for the developing countries. Trade is not sufficient to generate higher growth in these countries, and domestic factors are more important than economic openness. On the other hand, many studies have shown that trade openness does promote economic development. The effects of portfolio and foreign direct investments are also debated in the literature. Although the earlier dependency arguments and the later contagious financial crises in the 1990s led to varying degrees of opposition or reservation concerning capital market integration, there have been equally strong, if not stronger, theoretical arguments and empirical evidence showing that financial and production capital market integration benefits the economic development of countries in general.

Economic development ... removes an incentive for ... citizens to engage in transnational terrorist incidents.

Although it is certainly not feasible to expect to settle definitely the controversy over the effect of economic openness on development, it suffices to note that the possible negative effect of economic globalization on transnational terrorism may be achieved by promoting economic development for the purpose of this analysis. The negative effect may be realized through two channels. As a country expands its trade, FDI [foreign direct investment], and financial capital, its growing integration into the global economy arguably improves not only its own economic conditions but also those of its economic partner countries. Economic development in its own national economy removes an incentive for its citizens to engage in transnational terrorist incidents against foreign targets within the country. In addition, economic progress in its major partner countries reduces the likelihood that their citizens will cross borders to this country to engage in terrorist activities. If economic globalization promotes development, a country's economic integration affects simultaneously the development of itself and its major economic partners. Although a country's own development and that of its major partners affect transnational terrorist incidents inside the country, following the same theoretical logic, their effects are distinct empirically and should be separated in analysis.

8

Poverty Does Not Cause Terrorism

Walter Laqueur

Walter Laqueur has written The Age of Terrorism, The New Terrorism, *and* No End to War: Terrorism in the Twenty-First Century. *He works for the Center for Strategic and International Studies in Washington, D.C.*

The claim that poverty gives rise to terrorism is widely made. However, terrorist activity actually rarely occurs in the least developed countries. Even when it does, the terrorists themselves are often not natives, but outsiders from other nations. While it is true that some terrorist groups draw their membership from the lower classes, in other cases, terrorism seems to be a middle-class movement. Although poverty may certainly be a factor in terrorism, there are other more important factors, such as ethnic tensions and the personal psychology of terrorists.

It has been widely argued that a direct correlation exists between terrorism and poverty—that poverty, especially in what used to be called the third world, is the most important factor responsible for terrorism. However, the historical evidence does not bear out such categorical statements. It stands to reason that if all mankind were to live in small countries, preferably in small cities, and if all human beings were well off, there would be less violence, be it crime or terrorism. But

Walter Laqueur, *No End to War: Terrorism in the Twenty-First Century.* New York: Continuum, 2003. Copyright © 2003 by Walter Laqueur. Reproduced by permission of The Continuum International Publishing Group.

there is no reason to assume that violence would disappear altogether.

Some European terrorist groups and some Islamists have claimed to act on behalf and in the interest of the poorest of the poor. But in the forty-nine countries currently designated by the United Nations as the least developed hardly any terrorist activity occurs. (Among the criteria underlying this list are not only low per-capita income but also weak human resources and a low level of economic diversification.) In the list of these countries, in particular those located in Africa (the majority), many have experienced major unrest such as civil war (e.g., Burundi, Somalia, and Sierra Leone) and others have fought against each other (Ethiopia and Eritrea), but only one in which terrorism played a certain role, namely, the Sudan. But in the Sudan too, it was not the native Sudanese element that played the main role but foreign terrorists who were hiding in the country and using it as a training ground. They had bought themselves into Sudan, which was relatively easy in view of the poverty of the country and the radical Islamic orientation of some of its leaders. The same situation prevailed in Eritrea. But these countries were not safe havens for terrorists; when the French made an offer, the Sudanese government turned over [international terrorist] Carlos, who was hiding in Sudan, and Eritrea released Ethiopian terrorists to Addis Ababa.

In the forty-nine countries currently designated by the United Nations as the least developed hardly any terrorist activity occurs.

The Sudanese rulers realized that the presence of foreign terrorists only caused trouble. The country was put on the list of "rogue states," and economic sanctions were taken. Furthermore, the Sudanese government was involved in a semipermanent war with the non-Muslim tribes in the south of the country and did not need further complications. [al Qaeda terrorist leader, Osama] Bin Laden, who was residing there and had heavily invested in the country, had to leave.

Terrorists from Developed Countries

What of other, somewhat more developed countries? From what classes of society were terrorists recruited? Was it not true that the grave economic problems facing countries such as Algeria or Pakistan, to name but two—a high birth rate and economic stagnation resulting in high unemployment, mainly among the young—created a fertile ground for terrorist movements? Again, the evidence in favor of the poverty argument is not conclusive. While the Irish Republican Army (IRA) has traditionally recruited its followers from the lower middle class and the working class, the Basque Euskadi Ta Azkatasuna (ETA) seems to have been composed mainly of young people of middle-class origin. Whereas Northern Ireland, the mainstay of the IRA, belonged to the less prosperous regions of the United Kingdom, the Basque provinces are among the most developed of Spain. In the Middle East, Palestinian [terrorist] groups such as Hamas, Islamic Jihad, and particularly the Lebanese Hizbullah are constituted to some extent of relatively poor people, but then the great majority of people in these societies are not wealthy. In any case, the leadership and the early Palestinian terrorists, such as the various popular fronts for the Liberation of Palestine, were strictly middle class, including one of their early heroines, Leila Khaled.

The Algerian Islamist terrorists came mainly from poor families, but the most militant such as the Egyptian and Saudi suicide bombers came from middle- or upper-middle-class families. Their parents were professional people, successful merchants, or belonged to the higher echelons of the bureaucracy. This applies in particular to the Bin Laden network, many of whose members were graduates of universities or technical high schools or military academies. The Egyptian terrorists concentrated their efforts for many years in the cities of Upper Egypt such as Assyut and Minya, which belonged to the more neglected regions of the country, but within that area they looked for their recruits among families who were better off and in particular university students. Ahmed Sheikh, London-born and sentenced to death in Pakistan for the murder of journalist Daniel Pearl, came from a well-to-do family and was educated at private schools, but was thrown out from two of them, which tends to point to more than average psychological trouble.

Terrorists Can Come from Almost Anywhere

This phenomenon, the appeal of terrorism to students with a middle-class background, has been observed for a long time in other parts of the world. [Political science expert] Ernst Halperin noted with regard to Latin American terrorism in the 1970s that if one were to apply a Marxist class analysis it would appear that terrorism was a movement of middle-class students against entrenched oligarchies, looking for an improvement in their status and their prospects as well as for political power.

With regard to Latin American terrorism in the 1970s ... it would appear that terrorism was a movement of middle-class students.

The European terrorist groups of the extreme left in Europe were predominantly middle class (more in Germany than in Italy), whereas those of the extreme right—neo-Nazis and skinheads—belonged to a lower social stratum. Shining Path in Peru was definitely a movement of the poor, but the Tamil Tigers in Sri Lanka was not. In brief, one would look in vain for a clear socioeconomic pattern in the composition of terrorist movements. Terrorism rarely occurs in the poorest and richest countries, especially if these happen to be small societies in which there is little anonymity; between these extremes, terrorism can occur almost anywhere.

It has been argued that the leadership of revolutionary movements has always been constituted by the elite. Marx after all did not come from a poor family. Engels owned a factory, and the prophet Muhammad, having married a wealthy widow, was well-off too. But radical Islamic terrorism is not a movement aiming at social revolution. While support for al Qa'ida was strong among the poor in Pakistan, there are obvious reasons that the militants should come from the middle class, even the upper middle class. A contemporary terrorist operating outside his own country has to be educated, have some technical competence, and be able to move without attracting attention in alien societies. In brief, such a person will have to have an education that cannot be found among the poor in Pakistani or Egyptian villages or Palestinian refugee camps, only among relatively well-off town folk. . . .

Why Poverty Is Not a Major Factor in Terrorism

While poverty is sometimes a contributing factor to the emergence and spread of terrorism, national-ethnic tensions are of considerably greater relevance, and much of the present study is devoted to this topic. Such conflicts were at the bottom of the confrontation in Kashmir, in Israel/Palestine, in Chechnya, and in Sri Lanka. They were not a decisive factor in some of the bloodiest terrorist campaigns, such as in Algeria, Colombia, or Central Asia. In other words, resolving national conflicts would be no more of a universal panacea to end terrorism than eradicating poverty. Solving national conflicts and reducing tensions between various ethnic groups remain vital aims but would not provide a magic wand. People who practice terrorism are extremists, not moderates, and the demands of extremists can hardly ever be satisfied without impairing the rights of other ethnic groups, especially if two groups happen to claim the same region or country. . . .

Hence it is important to consider psychological factors such as aggression and fanaticism, which are frequently neglected or even ignored in the terrorist context. They are neglected because they are much more difficult to define. While it is always possible to point to ways and means to deal with "objective factors," the psychological motives involved are far more elusive, far more difficult to confront. Such investigations are also neglected because they are repugnant to many as they tend to reduce the importance of the ideological factor in terrorism and lump together terrorists with other individuals showing high degrees of violence and aggression—such as serial murderers. Furthermore, if a strong biological-genetic base were proved, this might lead to a climate of hopelessness, for while there are ways and means to reduce unemployment and defuse national conflicts, there is no known cure at the present time for fanaticism.

A contemporary terrorist operating outside his own country has to be educated.

The realization that "objective factors" and ideology are usually insufficient to explain the decision of individuals or groups to opt for terrorism has led to a preoccupation with psychological and biological factors: Is there such a thing as a "terrorist personality"?

Psychologists of various schools (behaviorists as well as psychoanalysts) have stressed the importance of childhood experiences. Geneticists have shown a correlation between violence, aggression, and biological genetic factors, while research has focused on the presence of an extra chromosome (Klinefelter's syndrome), on serotonin and testosterone levels, and on the presence of toxic heavy metals and certain brain defects. But however interesting these studies, causation has no more been established than in the case of the objective factors; a great many people may have elevated serotonin and low cholesterol levels and yet do not become terrorists—and vice versa.

Minority Groups and Terrorism

The Irish patriots of the nineteenth and twentieth centuries fought for national independence, but their activities cannot explain why other minorities in Europe (even inside the United Kingdom, such as the Scots) did not choose terrorism as their strategy. Why did the radical Basque opt for terrorism whereas the Catalans, also a minority in Spain albeit a more numerous one, did not? Why did the Chechen engage in violent actions, but not the Tatars or other Muslim minorities in Russia? Why did the Tamil Tigers in Sri Lanka opt for terrorism and engage in one of the most protracted and bloody campaigns whereas the Muslims in Sri Lanka have not? And why have the Tamils in Southern India, far more numerous than those in Sri Lanka, been satisfied with their status and not carried out a war for total independence? Many hundred national and religious minorities in the world are persecuted and discriminated against; in fact there are few countries in which minorities do not believe that they are unfairly treated.

9

Poverty Causes Environmental Degradation

Jack M. Hollander

Jack M. Hollander is a professor of energy and resources at the University of California, Berkeley. He is the author of The Real Environmental Crisis *and* The Energy-Environment Connection.

While affluence is often blamed for environmental degradation, poverty is the true cause. The poor, in an effort to survive, overuse resources and pollute their environment. Affluence, on the other hand, actually fosters environmentalism. For example, in the United States, conservationism did not become popular until society achieved affluence after World War II and people had the time, energy, and funds to demand a cleaner environment. Citizens welcomed legislation and private initiatives designed to reverse environmental degradation. This history shows that as today's poor become affluent, they too will become environmentally conscious, and will be able to take advantage of conservation technologies that have already been developed.

Can you remember a day when you opened your morning newspaper *without* finding a dramatic and disturbing story about some environmental crisis that's either here already or lurks just around the corner? That would be a rare day. On one day the story may be about global warming; on the next it may be about overpopulation or air pollution or resource depletion or species extinction or sea-level rise or nuclear waste or toxic substances in our food and water. Especially jarring is the implication in most of these stories that *you and I are the enemy*—that our affluent lifestyles are chiefly responsible for upsetting nature's balance; polluting our cities, skies, and oceans; and squandering the natural resources that sustain us. Unless we change our thoughtless and wasteful ways, we are reminded, the earth will become a very inhospitable place for ourselves and our progeny.

Environmental Pessimism

Such media reportage reflects the pervasive pessimism about the future that has become the hallmark of today's environmental orthodoxy. Its central theme is that the *affluent* society, by its very nature, is the *polluting* society—the richer we become, the more we consume the earth's scarce resources, the more we overcrowd the planet, the more we pollute the earth's precious land, air, and water. The clear implication of this viewpoint is that the earth was a better place before humans were around to despoil it.

Some people, even some environmental scientists, genuinely subscribe to this gloomy picture of the earth's future. I do not hold that they are necessarily uninformed, or naive, or unprofessional, or captive to special interests. But they are indeed pessimistic. I am more optimistic about the earth's environmental future, and I believe there is plenty of evidence to support an optimistic, though not cornucopian, view of the environmental future. . . .

Affluence Fosters Environmentalism

In my judgment, people are not the enemy of the environment. Nor is affluence the enemy. Affluence does not inevitably foster environmental degradation. Rather, affluence fosters *environmentalism*. As people become more affluent, most become increasingly sensitive to the health and beauty of their environment. And gaining affluence helps provide the economic means to protect and enhance the environment. Of course, affluence alone does not guarantee a better environment. A sense of social responsibility is also required. Political will is also required. *But affluence is a key ingredient for ensuring a livable and sustainable environment for the future.*

The real enemy of the environment is *poverty*—the tragedy of billions of the world's inhabitants who face hunger, disease, and ignorance each day of their lives. Poverty is the environmental villain; poor people are its victims. Impoverished people often do plunder their resources, pollute their environment, and overcrowd their habitats. They do these things not out of willful neglect but only out of the need to survive. They are well aware of the environmental amenities that affluent people enjoy, but they also know that for them the journey to a better environment will be long and that their immediate goal must be to escape from the clutches of poverty. They cannot navigate this long journey without assistance—assistance from generous institutions, nations, and individuals and from sincere and effective policies of their own governments.

Poverty is the environmental villain; poor people are its victims.

For the affluent nations to assist people in the developing world is socially responsible and morally right. But from an environmental perspective the issue is more than ethical. It is pragmatic as well, since the environmental self-interests of the affluent would be well served by the eradication of poverty. This idea disturbs those who fear that people emerging from poverty will inevitably become "wasteful" consumers like ourselves and will only exacerbate the globe's environmental damage as they pursue the trappings of the good life. The fear is understandable, but the conclusion is wrong. Without doubt, people tasting affluence will embrace consumerism and become proud owners of property, vehicles, computers, cell phones, and the like. But they will also pursue education, good health, and leisure for themselves and their families. And *they will become environmentalists.*

Environmentalists Are Made

Environmentalists are made, not born. In the industrial countries environmentalism arose as a reaction to the negative impacts of early industrialization and economic growth. On the way from subsistence to affluence, people developed a greater sense of social responsibility and had more time and energy to reflect about environmental quality. They had experienced environmental deterioration firsthand, and they demanded improvement. One of the great success stories of the recent half-century is, in fact, the remarkable progress the industrial societies have made, during a period of robust economic growth, in reversing the negative environmental impacts of industrialization. In the United States the air is cleaner and the drinking water purer than at any time in five decades; the food supply is more abundant and safer than ever before; the forested area is the highest in three hundred years; most rivers and lakes are clean again; and, largely because of technological innovation and the information revolution, industry, buildings, and transportation systems are more energy- and resource-efficient than at any time in the past. This is not to say that the resource/environment situation in the United States is near perfect or even totally satisfactory—of course it is not. Much more needs to be done. But undeniably, the improvements have been remarkable. They have come about in a variety of ways—through government regulation, through taxation, through financial incentives, through community actions. Most important, these environmental improvements cannot be credited solely to government, environmental organizations, or lobbyists, though each has played an important role. Rather, they have come about because the majority of citizens in this and every other democratic affluent society demands a clean and livable environment. Does this imply that the affluent have achieved an improved environment in their own lands by exporting their pollution to the lands of the poor? That has rarely been the case. . . .

The Birth of Environmentalism

In its early years, the United States retained the continent's historically agrarian character, with a largely pastoral and wooded landscape from "sea to shining sea." By the mid-nineteenth century industrialization was sweeping the country, and a growing population, mostly recent immigrants, was enjoying unprecedented economic opportunities provided by the new manufacturing culture. But along with the gains from industrialization, people living and working in nineteenth-century urban areas of the United States and Britain were also experiencing signs of environmental deterioration. Cities were becoming overcrowded, skies and rivers were becoming polluted, and urban dwellers increasingly faced the twin killers of respiratory and intestinal diseases from air and water pollution.

One of the great success stories of the recent half-century is . . . reversing the negative environmental impacts of industrialization.

Yet it was rural, not urban, pollution that stimulated the awakening of an American environmental movement. The first American "environmentalists" were an elite group of amateur naturalists who were disturbed by the changes to the pristine rural environment accompanying the country's industrial development—leveling of forests, overrunning of open spaces, invading of wilderness areas. Among the most idealistic of these naturalists was John Muir, who worked tirelessly for the total preservation of wilderness areas and old forests, mostly in the mountainous areas of the far West, with the hope that future generations would be able to experience the grandeur of these precious natural resources just as he experienced them. The first head of the Sierra Club (1892), Muir has rightly been called "the father of the national park system." Equally dedicated but often at loggerheads with Muir was America's first professional forester, Gifford Pinchot, who believed not in hands-off preservation but in the sustainable use of natural resources through wise management. Becoming the leader of the utilitarian wing of the conservation movement, Pinchot was appointed the first head of the U.S. Forest Service (1905) by President Theodore Roosevelt. Roosevelt was a strong and consistent ally of the conservationists, though his dedication to preserving the habitats of wild animals was due at least partly to his passion for hunting them. Drawing on the leadership of such individuals, some of the world's foremost environmental organizations, including the Sierra Club and the World Wildlife Fund, were formed, and they played a critical role during those early decades in winning public support for nature conservation.

Pollution became a symbol . . . of growing prosperity and an abundance of jobs.

In contrast to their early sensitivity about the rural environment, Americans generally tolerated urban pollution for another half-century. Not only was urban pollution initially perceived as an inevitable by-product of industrial production, but in the twentieth century's first two decades pollution became a symbol, at least among the working classes, of growing prosperity and an abundance of jobs. And during the Great Depression years of the 1930s, when massive unemployment returned and poverty became a fact of life for millions of Americans, chimney smoke and soot from still-operating industries became an even more welcome urban sight. Smoke in the air meant food on the table, at least for those who had jobs.

With the coming of World War II, the economic situation abruptly improved, but the environment did not. The wartime economy generated enormous production increases, full employment, and even higher levels of air and water pollution. After the war, the return to peacetime production brought an unprecedented surge of affluence and a seemingly insatiable demand for homes, automobiles, and other consumer products that had been unavailable in wartime. The pollution, unfortunately, only worsened.

Environmental Awareness in the Twentieth Century

But soon another kind of demand was stirring. Along with the new affluence and consumer demand, a heightened level of environmental awareness gradually evolved among the general public. This had no precedent in the earlier conservation movement, which was largely confined to a rural elite. The burgeoning postwar American middle class wanted their cities and neighborhoods to reflect their new affluence, to be attractive and healthy places to live. By the 1950s high levels of urban pollution that had been tolerated before and during the war became unacceptable to more and more Americans. By then it was no longer a laughing matter when the Cuyahoga River in Cleveland burst into flames because its surface was covered with industrial debris and slime. Or when the skies over Los Angeles became so smoggy that one could "see" the air but not the ground. Or when residents of an upstate New York community discovered that their homes had been knowingly built over an old industrial waste dump and were being threatened by leakage of toxic materials. The desire to find environmental quality at an affordable price was in fact one of the main stimuli for the exodus of millions of Americans from decaying core cities to the newly developing, still pristine suburbs.

All over the country, people began demanding cleaner air, water, and land. By the start of the 1970s both federal and state governments responded to the public's voice by creating new executive agencies dedicated to environmental protection. A stream of environmental mandates and regulations soon emanated from these agencies and the legislatures, beginning a trend toward ever tighter environmental controls that continues to this day. Also proliferating during this period were nongovernmental organizations (NGOs) that focused on environmental issues, such as the Natural Resources Defense Council and the Environmental Defense Fund, which collectively soon constituted a powerful political force. These NGOs were influential in stimulating, often through legal actions, many government policies and regulations that were to play an essential role in reducing pollution. It is important to keep in mind that these environmental responses were not forced on people. Overwhelmingly, Americans have supported both government regulations and private initiatives to improve the environment. And organized environmental activism was by no means confined to the United States. Similar activities and initiatives were occurring in all the industrial countries of the noncommunist world, as a result of which thousands of environmental interest groups and NGOs function throughout the world today. . . .

A Healthy Economy Is Good for the Environment

With history as our guide, we can be confident that today's poor peoples, as they begin climbing the economic ladder and enjoying some measures of freedom, will attend first to basic personal and family problems of sustenance and health, just as yesterday's poor did. With the increase of freedom and affluence—both are crucial—people are then likely to become motivated and increasingly able to apply the necessary political will, economic resources, and technological ingenuity to address environmental issues more broadly.

Overwhelmingly, Americans have supported both government regulations and private initiatives to improve the environment.

Despite much rhetoric to the contrary, there is no inherent conflict between a healthy economy and environmental quality; actually they go hand in hand. Is it not persuasive that for decades the robust economic growth of the affluent societies has coincided with their continuing environmental improvement? For the future, a major key to environmental quality, for both the emerging and industrial economies, will be development and use of innovative technologies that are *both* economically attractive and environmentally friendly. Fortunately, today's developing societies hold a tremendous advantage over yesterday's. They do not need to tread through the entire learning experience in each technology area; instead they can "leapfrog" over the pathways (and mistakes) of the industrial pioneers and jump straightaway to the environmentally kinder and smarter technologies of the twenty-first century.

Environmental Fears Are Not Justified

There is also little basis for the fear that worldwide economic development will bring about massive environmental deterioration from the newly affluent becoming unrestrained consumers imitating the technology-oriented ways of the rich. In this century consumerism can increasingly mean replacing old and polluting technologies with new, resource-efficient and environmentally friendly technologies. Technological innovation and economic efficiency—the major keys to environmental quality—can be expected to take root increasingly in the developing nations as they make the transition to democracy and affluence. Supported by new technologies and management arrangements, agriculture, fishing, and manufacturing in the developing world have the potential eventually to become resource efficient and environmentally sustainable. As our knowledge increases, an increasing awareness of the importance of healthy ecosystems—a critical factor to achieving a sustainable environment—can be expected to develop among people everywhere. Gradually, both the poor and the rich will reduce the unwise use of forests and other natural resources, as all people progress toward affluence and democratic choice.

Nor is the fear justified that development will bring with it unsustainable exploitation of energy resources. Although it is clear that economic growth will bring about substantial increases in demand for energy *services* (such as transportation, heating, lighting, and information processing), the growth in actual energy-resource consumption can be considerably reduced by efficiency gains of the technologies supplying both energy and energy services. (For example, compact fluorescent lightbulbs, still in their infancy in terms of technical development and consumer acceptance, use only a quarter as much electricity as standard incandescent bulbs.) The amounts of fossil fuels consumed will continue to increase for several decades because of technological inertia, but in the longer term cleaner and more efficient energy technologies will become economically accessible in the developing world, and these have the potential to reduce greatly the pollution problems traditionally associated with fossil fuel burning. Another example: millions more vehicles will be on the roads in the developing countries, but they will be tomorrow's high-tech low polluters rather than yesterday's low-tech high polluters.

10

Poverty Does Not Cause Environmental Degradation

David Satterthwaite

David Satterthwaite is a senior fellow at the International Institute for Environment and Development in London.

There is a worldwide trend toward increasingly urbanized cities. With this trend have come increased poverty rates. While the poor are often blamed for environmental degradation, they actually contribute little to it. The poor do face environmental hazards such as inadequate water, sanitation, and drainage. However, these hazards do not degrade any environmental resource. By contrast, urban development overuses resources such as fossil fuels, freshwater, soil, and forests, and urban centers generate high levels of biodegradable waste. The poor, on the other hand, use far fewer of these resources and produce less waste because they are the primary recyclers.

The need to understand and act on poverty-environment linkages in urban areas becomes all the more imperative as urban populations (and the number living in poverty,) grow and as the contribution of urban-based production and urban consumption to environmental degradation increases. By 2000, approximately two-fifths of Africa's and Asia's population and three-quarters of Latin America's population lived in urban areas. The trend is toward increasingly urbanized so-

David Satterthwaite, "The Links Between Poverty and the Environment in Urban Areas of Africa, Asia, and Latin America," *The Annals of the American Academy of Political and Social Sciences,* vol. 590 Annals 73, November 2003, pp. 73–86. Copyright © by the American Academy of Political and Social Science. Reproduced by permission of Sage Publications, Inc.

cieties in most countries as most new investment is urban-based; as the [UN's] Brundtland Commission's report *Our Common Future* remarked, "the future will be predominantly urban and the most immediate environmental concerns of most people will be urban ones".

Africa, Asia, and Latin America also have nearly three-quarters of the world's urban population and most of the world's largest and fastest-growing cities. How these urban centers perform in terms of resource use and waste generation has very large implications for sustainable development within their regions and globally. But in these regions, increasing urbanization levels have also been characterized by growing numbers of people living in poverty. More than 600 million urban dwellers live in shelters and neighborhoods where their lives and health are continually threatened because of poor quality, overcrowded housing, and inadequate provision of safe water supplies, sanitation, drainage, and garbage collection. Most of this population lives in squatter settlements or illegal subdivisions where the housing is makeshift and largely constructed of temporary materials or in tenements or cheap boarding houses with high levels of overcrowding. Typically, the inhabitants face multiple deprivations—inadequate food intakes; large health burdens from the illnesses and injuries associated with very poor-quality homes and inadequate water, sanitation, and garbage collection; inadequacies in public transport; difficulties in getting health care and affording medicines; difficulties (and often high costs) of keeping children at school; long hours worked; and the often dangerous working conditions. Many face a constant risk of violence and are threatened with eviction. Many are particularly vulnerable to extreme weather—to flooding because they live on floodplains or beside rivers, to landslides for those living on slopes. Of course, the scale and relative importance of these vary from person to person and place to place, but large sections of the urban population in virtually all low- and middle-income nations face a mix of these deprivations.

The Relationship Between Urban Poverty and Environmental Degradation

It is often assumed that urban poverty is linked to environmental degradation or even that it is a major cause of environmental degradation. This article describes how this is not so. Indeed, the key relationship between environmental degradation and urban development is in regard to the consumption patterns of nonpoor urban groups (especially high-income groups) and the urban-based production and distribution systems that serve them. Ironically, at a continental or global level, high levels of urban poverty in Africa, Asia, and Latin America (which also means low levels of consumption, resource use, and waste generation) have helped to keep down environmental degradation. . . .

Increasing urbanization levels have also been characterized by growing numbers of people living in poverty.

At the core of most misunderstandings about the link between poverty and environment is the confusion between environmental hazards and environmental degradation. In most urban centers in Africa, Asia, and Latin America, a high proportion of the poor (however defined) face very serious environmental hazards in their homes and their surrounds and in their workplaces. Such hazards impose large burdens on such groups in terms of ill health, injury, and premature death. These health burdens are a major cause or contributor to poverty. But most of these environmental hazards are not causing environmental degradation. For instance, the inadequacies in provision for piped water, sanitation, and drainage in most low-income neighborhoods often mean very serious problems with insect-borne diseases such as malaria or dengue fever or filariasis and with diseases associated with a lack of water for washing such as trachoma, but these do not degrade any environmental resource.

Environmental Degradation and Poverty

There are four different kinds of environmental degradation associated with urban development: the first is high use or waste of nonrenewable resources—including the consumption of fossil fuels. There is little association between this and poverty since most poor urban dwellers have very low consumption levels for nonrenewable resources. Most of the houses in which they live (and often build for themselves) make widespread use of recycled or reclaimed materials and little use of cement and other materials with a high-energy input. Such households have too few capital goods to represent much of a draw on the world's finite reserves of metals and other nonrenewable resources. Most low-income groups rely on public transport (or travel by foot or bicycle), which ensures low averages for oil consumption per person. Low-income households on average have low levels of electricity consumption, not only because those who are connected use less but also because a high proportion of households have no electricity supply.

The second is high use of the renewable resources for which there are finite limits—for instance, fresh water, soil, and forests. Poor urban dwellers generally have much lower levels of consumption for renewable resources than middle- and upper-income groups. For instance, poor urban dwellers have much lower levels of consumption for fresh water (although this is due more to inconvenient and/or expensive supplies than to need or choice). They occupy much less land per person than middle- and upper-income groups. For instance, in Nairobi, the informal and illegal settlements that house more than half the city's population occupy less than 6 percent of the land area used for residential purposes. Urban sprawl, which often means paving over very high-quality agricultural land, is far more the result of the residential preferences of middle- and upper-income groups, new commercial and industrial developments, and city-transport programs dominated by highway construction than of land occupation by low-income groups.

There are examples of low-income populations contributing to the degradation of some renewable resources such as low-income settlements developed in watersheds—but this is not so much a problem of poor groups' causing degradation as a problem caused by the failure of urban authorities to ensure that they have access to other residential sites.

The urban poor generally have a very positive role from an ecological perspective.

A third kind of environmental degradation associated with urban areas is high levels of biodegradable waste generation, which overtax the capacities of renewable sinks (e.g., the capacity of a river to break down biodegradable wastes without ecological degradation). Low-income groups usually generate much lower levels per person than middle- and upper-income groups and thus contribute much less to the environmental degradation caused by the dumping of untreated wastes into water bodies and poorly managed waste dumps. In fact, the urban poor generally have a very positive role from an ecological perspective, as they are the main reclaimers, reusers, and recyclers of wastes from industries, workshops, and wealthier households. Some small-scale urban enterprises . . . can cause serious local environmental problems, such as the contamination of local water sources. But these enterprises' contribution to citywide pollution problems relative to other groups is usually very small. In addition, it is difficult to ascribe the pollution caused by small-scale enterprises to the urban poor when many such enterprises are owned by middle- or upper-income groups.

The fourth kind of environmental degradation associated with urban areas is high levels of generation of nonbiodegradable wastes/emissions that overtax the (finite) capacity of local and global sinks to absorb or dilute them without adverse effects (e.g., the use of persistent pesticides and the generation of greenhouse gases and stratospheric ozone-depleting chemicals). Low-income groups generally contribute very little to their generation either directly (through the fuels they use and goods they consume) or indirectly (through the environmental costs created by the fabrication of the goods they use). For instance, in regard to greenhouse gas emissions, low-income groups usually generate much lower levels per person than middle- and upper-income groups because their use of fossil fuels or of goods or services with high fossil-fuel inputs is much lower. The only exception may be in urban areas where there is a need for space heating for parts of the year and a proportion of the urban poor use biomass fuels or coal in inefficient stoves or fires. This may result in these households' having above-average per capita contributions to carbon dioxide emissions (and also to urban air pollution), but these are exceptional cases, and in general, the consumption patterns of low-income groups imply much lower greenhouse gas emissions per person than those of middle- and upper-income groups.

11

Education for the Poor Must Be Improved

Benjamin L. Page and James R. Simmons

Benjamin L. Page is the author or coauthor of several books, including Who Gets What from Government, The Rational Public, *and* What Government Can Do. *He is a professor of political science at Northwestern University. James R. Simmons directs the public administration program at the University of Wisconsin, Oshkosh. He is also a professor and chair of the university's Department of Political Science.*

Providing education and job training to the poor is essential for helping them escape poverty. Although public education is one of the triumphs of American democracy, the segregation of schools along lines of social class and race has led to inferior education for poor students. While there has been some progress made toward providing equal funding to schools with poor students, equal funding is not enough to make up for the disadvantages poor students face. Some of the greatest harms of segregation are not the financial aspects, they are the social aspects. Segregation creates low self-esteem, eliminates interpersonal networks, and decreases job prospects. Although formal legal segregation was eliminated in the 1960s, residential segregation has kept schools from becoming fully integrated. Since integration makes a differ-

ence in the quality of education for students, if it cannot be accomplished, resources superior to those provided to better-off schools must be provided to poor schools to compensate.

In dealing with poverty and inequality, it makes sense to put a high priority on training and education. So long as people's incomes are largely determined by the outcome of labor markets, the "human capital" that they carry within themselves—their skills, talents, work habits, and even their energy and aspirations—is crucial to the wages and salaries that they will earn. Human capital strongly affects the quality and quantity of work that people can do, which in turn strongly affects their incomes. And human capital is largely a result of education and training.

If we want people to rise out of *poverty*, therefore, a very natural strategy is to make sure that they get good education and job training so they can do valuable work that will earn them substantial incomes. It would be unrealistic to imagine that *all* poverty could be eradicated in this way (training cannot always overcome severe physical or mental disabilities, for example), but a great deal could be accomplished.

By the same token, education is absolutely critical to the idea of *equal opportunity*. If people are to have an "equal chance" to achieve economic well-being, they need to start the competitive race with equal skills and talents. In the information age, physical strength and stamina may no longer be so necessary, but cognitive and verbal skills are essential. To the extent that people are born significantly unequal or fall behind in infancy due to bad luck in their choice of parents and home environment, therefore, substantial *compensatory* education may be necessary in order to provide them with any semblance of an equal start. It is also important to work directly to prevent disadvantages of birth, nutrition, and health from taking their toll before formal schooling begins . . . .

Elementary and Secondary Schools

The provision of free, universal elementary and secondary school education has long been seen as a great triumph of American democracy. In this instance, in contrast to most aspects of the welfare state, the United States has actually led the way. The U.S. system of public elementary schools was mostly in place by the last quarter of the nineteenth century, whereas England and other European countries continued bifurcated, largely private school systems into the twentieth century. The quicker U.S. start may have had to do with our need to build many new schools as western lands were settled, as well as the relative weakness of class divisions and the strength of a certain limited ideology of equality. In any case, urbanization, industrialization, immigration, and changes in the family (especially the development of a working class employed for wages outside the home), along with democratic politics and reformist institutions, led in most U.S. cities to full-fledged systems of public elementary schools that were age-graded, free, often compulsory, hierarchically organized, and taught and administered by professionals. High schools largely took their present form during the Great Depression of the 1930s, when job scarcity made it sensible for teenagers to stay in school.

For most of the last century, U.S. public schools have been widely praised for accomplishing many things: training an industrial workforce, helping "Americanize" immigrants from many foreign cultures, training Americans in democratic citizenship. Public schools have also been seen as providing a major ingredient of equal opportunity, educating the poor and those of modest means free of charge and doing so in *common schools* along with the well-off and people of diverse cultural backgrounds, all sharing a common curriculum.

Unequal Schooling

Recent historical research has cast doubt on just how golden the "golden age" of U.S. public education was, however. There were, for example, many class-related battles over local autonomy for working-class communities *versus* centralized control by upper-middle-class administrators and officials, and the latter generally won. And equality has always been achieved only within local areas, not among them. But more important, even local equality in public schooling soon began to break down. The common curriculum, for example, eroded in high schools after a 1918 National Education Association report advocated designing curricula to meet the needs of the new majority of students, most of whom were not going on to college. The subsequent fragmentation of courses, and eventually tracking, undoubtedly helped prepare students for the kinds of lives and work they were most likely to encounter, but it also limited schools' effects on social mobility and equality.

Recent historical research has cast doubt on just how golden the 'golden age' of U.S. public education was, however.

Over many decades, the ideal of the common school for diverse students—implemented by including everyone from a given residential area—also increasingly was thwarted by residential segregation along lines of ethnicity and social class. After World War II especially, affluent and middle-class whites, with help from government Federal Housing Administration loans and new federal highways, moved out of the cities into homogeneous suburbs with homogeneous and relatively affluent schools. They left working-class people, the poor, and minorities behind in inner cities, attending increasingly segregated and impoverished public schools. Today, for example, cities like Detroit, Cleveland, Gary, Milwaukee, and Chicago, with 25–40 percent minority populations, concentrate most of their African-American and Latino citizens into highly segregated neighborhoods. Affluent people who have stayed in central cities often send their children to expensive private schools that are generally unavailable to those of modest means.

"Savage Inequalities"

The result has been what [author] Jonathan Kozol called "savage inequalities." In contrast to the expansive facilities (good buildings, abundant libraries and computers), well-trained and well-rewarded teachers, and ambitious peers often found in affluent suburbs, many inner-city students have to cope with skimpy funding, decaying (sometimes dangerous) buildings, scarce supplies, burnt-out teachers, and segregated, demoralized fellow-students. Urban schools are often unhappy places. As [writer] Gene Maeroff, another sympathetic observer, has put it, the "dismal panorama" of urban schools leads to "withered hopes, stillborn dreams."

The data are clear. Schools with high concentrations of poor students tend to have older buildings that are more in need of maintenance, less qualified teachers, less challenging and advanced curricula, fewer books, fewer computers, and fewer Internet connections. Many classes with high enrollments of poor students are taught by out-of-field teachers who lack training in the subject. This is especially true of English and science. The question is what to do about unequal schooling.

Does Money Help?

Even completely equal funding would not bring equal education or equal opportunity. One focus has been financial: the big differences between the levels of income and wealth in different school districts, which—when schools rely on local property taxes—translates into gross inequalities in the amount of money available to schools. It is hard to argue that schools with widely varying resources can provide equal educational opportunities for all the children in a given state. Indeed, in the 1971 *Serrano* case, the California Supreme Court declared that such inequalities among districts in the Los Angeles area violated the guarantee of equal protection of the laws under both the state and the federal constitutions. . . .

Progress toward more equal funding is certainly welcome. But it is important to see that even completely equal funding would not bring equal education or equal opportunity because it takes *more* effort and more money per pupil to educate disadvantaged students. Making up for early childhood deprivation, dealing with non-English speakers, providing special education for children with disabilities—these things are very expensive. Moreover, disadvantages within a school are cumulative. The quality of peer support and peer pressure has been shown to have very strong effects on educational achievement. A student surrounded by eager, self-confident, proficient fellow-students simply has a much better chance to learn than one surrounded by the disadvantaged and discouraged. This is one reason why residential segregation is so pernicious. For these reasons, to provide disadvantaged students (and students surrounded by disadvantaged students) with equal chances for educational achievement requires not merely equal funding, but *compensatory* efforts involving more than equal resources.

Even completely equal funding would not bring equal education or equal opportunity.

Unfortunately, the post-*Serrano* drive for compensatory or at least equal educational resources has run into a surprising obstacle: the argument that money—or even the quality of schools themselves—does not really make any difference to educational achievement. It is said to be pointless to "throw money" at the problem. In recent years, this argument has been made with particular vigor by some who advocate a radical restructuring of education through vouchers or other forms of privatization. What should we make of it?

The Coleman Report

The "money doesn't matter" argument has roots in the first wave of systematic research, particularly the 1966 Coleman report on equality of educational opportunity, which concluded that the effects of money and of measured school inputs (facilities, curriculum, even teacher quality) had little or no impact on students' academic achievement. A host of subsequent studies have come up with conflicting estimates of the effects of school resources, often failing to find any statistically significant impact. As Larry Hedges and others have pointed out, however, the point is to calculate the *best* estimate of effects across a number of studies by some such technique as taking the *average* estimate—which is very large and positive.

Such estimates may be somewhat too large, due to publication biases (journals do not like nonfindings) and selection bias (parents who value education highly and help their children learn tend to choose to live in high-spending districts, making the spending seem responsible for success). Still, as schools have spent more money per pupil over the last two or three decades, the average achievement test scores of representative samples of students have mostly improved—though not by a lot, only for poor students, and about twice as much on math as reading. Estimates of spending effects based on changes over time, too, may be somewhat biased upward because parents' levels of education and income have risen (and the number of children per family has fallen), all tending independently to raise school achievement at the same time that school spending has risen. On the other hand, to the extent that spending is concentrated in the neediest areas, we should not be surprised at a lack of positive correlation of funding levels with achievement.

The arguments continue. Gary Burtless's volume of essays on this issue pessimistically concluded that differences in school resources—while they may improve students' later earnings prospects—have essentially no effects on academic achievement, and that increased spending on school inputs has "not been shown to be an effective way to improve student achievement" in most instances. We can agree that spending lots of money on schools is not a *sufficient* condition for improving achievement because it bound to matter exactly how the money is spent. Yet spending may well be a *necessary* condition for providing a good education. Surely a lack of habitable buildings, a dearth of reasonably paid teachers, or an absence of books and computers is not likely to advance educational aims. Surely it is easier to get excellent teachers if you pay them well. Research suggesting that *simply* "throwing money" at schools will not necessarily help should not be used as an excuse to deny books to the illiterate, to tolerate gross inequities, or to neglect the compensatory measures that are known to help poor students. Instead, questions about effects of money should encourage thinking about which factors matter most and where resources can have the most impact: perhaps in smaller class sizes, for example.

Segregation

It is easy to lose sight of one important fact that was emphasized in the Coleman Report and is agreed on by virtually all researchers: peers matter. Students are helped or harmed by the playmates, neighbors, and fellow-students who surround them. It follows inescapably that any educational system that segregates students by race, income level, or any other factor correlated with academic ability or achievement—any system that concentrates high-achieving students in some schools and low-achieving students in others—is bound to disadvantage the students who end up with below-average classmates. Besides affecting students schoolwork and cognitive skills, such segregation is likely to create inequalities in self-esteem, access to interpersonal networks, and job prospects.

In the case of race, the U.S. Supreme Court long ago ruled, in *Brown v. Board of Education* (1954), that state action deliberately bringing about racial segregation violates African Americans' rights to equal protection of the laws. Subsequent court decisions required states to dismantle segregation policies. The Civil Rights Act of 1964 put teeth into these decisions by denying federal aid (most notably under the subsequent Elementary and Secondary Education Act of 1965) to school districts that discriminate on the basis of race or other arbitrary grounds. Slowly, painfully, with much resistance and foot-dragging, formal legal segregation in the South was broken down. Black students were no longer forbidden to attend all-white schools, and single-race public schools were integrated, at least to a token extent.

Private Choices Continue Segregation

Almost immediately, however, private choices began to undo integration. Private, all-white "academies" were set up in the South to evade desegregation for those who could afford the tuition. In many parts of the country, there was "white flight": some parents chose residential locations (in lily-white suburbs, for example) partly to avoid sending their children to integrated schools. This did not always represent racism—some middle-class blacks fled as well. It sometimes represented "classism," a perceived self-interest in avoiding schools with many poor or disadvantaged students, for the reasons noted above. But the brutal fact of widespread *residential segregation*, regardless of motive, operated together with the long-standing system of *school attendance by location of residence* to reestablish segregated schools, not only in the South, but also in the cities and suburbs of the North. [Sociologists] Douglas Massey and Nancy Denton speak of "American apartheid."

Recognizing that residential segregation was perpetuating school segregation, and seeking to counteract it, the federal courts began ordering remedies like compulsory busing to non-neighborhood schools. The history of busing is painful to contemplate. There is some evidence that intelligently arranged busing can work well for students and gain acceptance by parents. But it does go against the obvious virtues of neighborhood schools (ease of transportation, encouragement of parental involvement, facilitation of after-school friendships). And fearful parents—their concerns sometimes inflamed by race-baiting politicians—created storms of protest and eventually forced the courts to retreat or legislatures to override busing plans. The result has been highly segregated schools, in which most minority students are surrounded mainly by minorities. In the mid-1990s, for example, some 73 percent of Hispanics attended public schools where more than half the students were Hispanic, and 65 percent of blacks attended public schools where more than half the students were black. Segregation by income and socioeconomic status is also extreme.

But the brutal fact of widespread residential segregation . . . operated . . . to reestablish segregated schools.

As long as we insist on both freedom of residential choice and residentially based school attendance, our public schools are likely to be heavily segregated by race and income. The segregated students are going to be harmed as a result. As [sociologist] Orlando Patterson points out, one logical reaction to the rejection of busing is to address the underlying problem of residential segregation and to work seriously to integrate our neighborhoods.

Integration Makes a Difference

Integration can make a difference. Quasi-experimental data from the Gatreaux program in Chicago (in which some African-American public housing tenants were randomly assigned to new housing in the city and some to the higher-income, mostly white suburbs) indicate that the children of suburban movers were considerably less likely to drop out of school and more likely to take college-track courses. They were much more likely to attend college (54 percent to 21 percent) and to attend a four-year college (27 percent to 4 percent).

But it is not easy to integrate with affluent whites on a large scale if they do not want to be integrated. The only other way to give disadvantaged students truly equal opportunities, in the sense of equal chances for high academic achievement, is to make special compensatory efforts. That means not merely providing resources equal to those in luckier schools and neighborhoods, but providing *superior* resources.

12

Rural Poverty Has Become Worse than Urban Poverty

Timothy Egan

Timothy Egan is a reporter for The New York Times. *He won the Pulitzer Prize in 2001.*

Rural communities are experiencing serious poverty, similar to what many inner cities went through in the 1960s and 1970s. This has led to increased crime and drug abuse, both linked to a methamphetamine epidemic in these communities. Those who work in honest employment are 60 percent more likely to earn minimum wage than workers in urban areas. As a result, people are leaving the poorest rural counties. However, most politicians have ignored these problems, choosing instead to focus on farm price supports as a means of aid, even though most rural jobs are nonagricultural. Other politicians are looking to a modern-day Homestead Act, which would encourage people to move to depressed rural areas, as a potential solution.

Loup County, Neb., the poorest county in the nation, is down to 712 people—a third of the population it had nearly a century ago. A four-bedroom house goes for $30,000. But building a life is much harder. In Loup County, what rides on the unrelenting winds are symptoms of despair that have taken hold there and across a large swath of rural America.

It could be Chemung County in upstate New York, which lost people and jobs even in the boom of the 90's. Or Bighorn County, Wyo., where some high school seniors say their only choices are to move out of town or take up with people cooking methamphetamine in a rusty sink. Or Dalhart, Tex., a Panhandle town of 7,000 people where the murder rate [in 2001] was more than twice the national average.

A Silent Rural Collapse

Around the country, rural ghettos are unravelling in the same way that inner cities did in the 1960's and 70's, according to the officials and experts who have tried to make sense of a generations-old downward spiral in the countryside. In this view, decades of economic decline have produced a culture of dependency, with empty counties hooked on farm subsidies just as welfare mothers were said to be tied to their monthly checks. And just as in the cities, the hollowed-out economy has led to a frightening rise in crime and drug abuse.

But unlike the cities' troubles, which generated a national debate about causes and solutions, the rural collapse has been largely silent, perhaps because it happened so slowly.

Crime, fueled by a methamphetamine epidemic that has turned fertilizer into a drug lab component and given some sparsely populated counties higher murder rates than New York City, has so strained small-town police budgets that many are begging the federal government for help. The rate of serious crime in Nebraska, Kansas, Oklahoma and Utah is as much as 50 percent higher than the state of New York, the F.B.I. reported in October [2002].

Towns of 10,000 and 25,000 people are now the most likely places to experience a bank robbery. Drug-related homicides fell by 50 percent in urban areas, but they tripled over the last decade in the countryside.

"We have serious drug crime in places that never used to have it," said Allen Curtis, executive director of the Nebraska Crime Commission.

Poverty was held in place somewhat by the boom of the 1990's. Still, the 2000 census found that the percentage of people living below the poverty level is nearly 30 percent higher in rural areas than it is in cities. Of the 25 poorest counties in the nation, 5 are in Nebraska, 5 are in Texas and 4 are in South Dakota, the Commerce Department found. In Loup County, the dead center of Nebraska, per capita personal income is $6,606 per year, just 22 percent of the national average, according to a listing compiled by the Commerce Department.

Equally telling is a growing wage gap that finds people who work in rural areas making just 70 percent of the average salaries of workers in urban areas. The cost of living, of course, is much lower outside the big cities. But workers in rural areas are 60 percent more likely to earn minimum wage than urban wage-earners.

No wonder then that the exodus from large parts of rural America is continuing, extending far beyond the long-suffering Great Plains. While the nation as a whole grew by 13 percent in the 2000 census, many counties in upstate New York, Pennsylvania, Ohio, Illinois, Michigan and three Southern states, for example, lost 9 percent or more of their population during the 1990's.

Towns of 10,000 and 25,000 people are now the most likely places to experience a bank robbery.

The pastoral farms of cider presses and pumpkin patches still exist, of course, but the ones that prosper are at suburban edges, or they are places with sublime scenery or an energetic college. Bonner County, Idaho, for example, grew by 38 percent in the last decade, hooking its fate to outdoor amenities and second homes for early-retiring baby boomers.

Though the politicians who inveighed against moral and economic decline in the big cities have yet to weigh in on rural breakdown, plenty of voices are sounding alarms from this Other America.

Some say that entrepreneurship has been stifled by central government subsidies to agribusiness, while the real problems of rural America—which have little to do with farm policy—have been ignored.

"The slide is not inevitable," said Chuck Hassebrook, director of the Center for Rural Affairs in Walthill, Neb., a nonprofit group that studies trends in rural areas. "We give a lot of tax breaks and direct payments to big agriculture companies that don't do much for the local economy, but rarely do we give anything to the little guy trying to start a business and stay in town."

In Nebraska, nearly 70 percent of all farmers rely on government largess to stay in business. Yet the biggest economic collapse is happening in counties most tied to agriculture—in spite of the subsidies.

Methamphetamine in Rural Areas

Unaffected by the downward trends are cheap labs used to make methamphetamine, a synthetic form of speed that the White House calls the fastest-growing drug threat in America.

Nationwide, meth use has nearly tripled since 1994, and there are now far more regular users of meth than crack, according to the annual survey of drug use done for the National Institute on Drug Abuse.

In Wyoming, the least populated state, officials estimate that 1 out of every 100 people needs treatment for meth addiction. Users of meth tend to be white and rural. There were 300 times more seizures of meth labs in Iowa in 1999, for example, than in New York and New Jersey combined, the Drug Enforcement [Administration] found.

Like crack, meth drives up all the other problems in these communities. Meth users tend to be erratic, violent and in some cases, borderline psychotic—especially when on a sleepless binge, or "tweaking" episode. Small-fry dealers steal and war among one another. Users abandon families, lose jobs and batter spouses and loved ones.

There were 300 times more seizures of meth labs in Iowa in 1999 . . . than in New York and New Jersey combined.

"Meth seems to be everywhere in Nebraska right now," Mr. Curtis of the Nebraska Crime Commission said. "It's mostly Beavis and Butthead labs, with poor white kids making meth out of their cars."

Whether people would be less prone to using meth if there were more good-paying jobs in rural areas is an echo of an old question—the one posed about crack and heroin use in gutted inner cities. But at least during the decline-of-cities phase, the topic was vigorously debated.

By contrast, the problems of rural America were not discussed much in the recent national election [in 2002], even in South Dakota and Missouri, which had close Senate races.

Farm Price Supports

Instead, the issue was farm price supports. In South Dakota, which received $3.2 billion in farm subsidies [from 1997 to 2002] and stands to gain an even larger amount in the coming decade, candidates of both parties swore to uphold the status quo. Supporters of subsidies say they keep entire counties from going under and ensure a cheap and abundant food supply.

But opponents say that the biggest checks go to large corporate farms and do little to stem rural decline. The farm bill signed in May [2002] by President Bush—and backed by both parties—will, over the next 10 years, distribute two-thirds of $125 billion in payments to the top 10 percent of farms, according to an analysis by the Environmental Working Group, a conservation group.

These payments go to farm businesses that cannot make money in the global market without government help, or they are funneled to people who agree to take certain crops out of production.

But farmers who are just getting by tend to be out of the subsidy loop. About 1.2 million of the nation's 2 million farms do less than $10,000 a year in annual sales, the Agriculture Department reports.

Opponents say that the biggest checks go to large corporate farms and do little to stem rural decline.

In any case, with barely 1 percent of Americans living on farms, most rural jobs are nonagricultural. About 25 percent of those jobs pay wages below the poverty level for a family of four, said Representative Eva Clayton, a Democrat of South Carolina who is retiring [in 2002], and who served as chairwoman of the Congressional Rural Caucus.

Or, she said, more often the rural wage-earner makes a long commute to a minimum-wage job in the nearest regional hub city.

Jump-Starting Business and Population Growth

There are some bright spots on the open map. In some regional hubs, like Fargo, N.D., wages and jobs have increased. Across the Midwest, a number of communities have attracted enough immigrants to show population growth. But these immigrants come to work at meatpacking plants or corporate hog farms. And recent studies have shown those jobs tend to drive out other people who might normally stay in an area for its quality of life.

Representative Tom Osborne, Republican of Nebraska, has been trying to get small "action" grants—somewhat similar to the ones the big cities used to go after—as a way to jump-start businesses in western Nebraska.

In desperation, other rural politicians are looking to an earlier model.

Two major homestead acts were largely responsible for people moving to some of the least populated areas to begin with. Now comes the New Homestead Economic Opportunity Act, introduced by Senators Byron L. Dorgan, Democrat of North Dakota, and Chuck Hagel, Republican of Nebraska. The bill would forgive student loans and provide tax credit for home purchasers in depressed rural areas and small towns.

History has provided us a model to help the communities that are hurting in the heartland, Senator Dorgan said.

But history, at least since the end of the last homestead act around 1920, has also shown that people who live in depressed rural America have been going only one way—out.

Organizations to Contact

American Enterprise Institute for Public Policy (AEI)
1150 Seventeenth St. NW, Washington, DC   20036
(202) 862-5800 • fax: (202) 862-7177
e-mail: info@aei.org
Web site: www.aei.org

The institute is committed to preserving and strengthening limited government, private enterprise, strong foreign policy, and national defense. AEI's research covers economics and trade; social welfare; government tax, spending, regulatory, and legal policies; international affairs; and U.S. defense and foreign policies. Free articles, reports, and books are available on its Web site.

America's Second Harvest
35 E. Wacker Dr., Suite 2000, Chicago, IL   60601
(312) 263-2303
Web site: www.secondharvest.org

America's Second Harvest is the nation's largest domestic charitable hunger-relief organization. Its network includes more than two hundred regional food banks and serves more than 23 million Americans.

The Aspen Institute
One Dupont Circle NW, Suite 700
   Washington, DC   20036-1133
(202) 736-5800 • fax: (202) 467-0790
Web site: www.aspeninstitute.org

The Aspen Institute seeks to foster enlightened leadership, open-minded dialogue, and nonpartisan inquiry. It researches topics such as homeland security, education and society, health and biomedical science, and globalization. It publishes a quarterly magazine, the *Aspen Idea,* available on its Web site.

Borgen Project
e-mail: info@borgenproject.org
Web site: www.borgenproject.org

The Borgen Project is a nonpartisan organization committed to ending poverty in the United States and abroad. It advocates for awareness of the Millennium Development Goals and for better health care for American veterans. Its Web site offers information on poverty worldwide.

The Brookings Institution
1775 Massachusetts Ave. NW
  Washington, DC   20036-2188
(202) 797-6000 • fax: (202) 797-6004
e-mail: brookinfo@brookings.edu
Web site: www.brookings.edu

This nonpartisan institution is one of Washington, D.C.'s, oldest think tanks. Its research and publications cover economics, government, foreign policy, and the social sciences. It publishes the quarterly journal the *Brookings Review* as well as books and policy briefs.

Cato Institute
1000 Massachusetts Ave. NW
  Washington, DC   20001-5403
(202) 842-0200 • fax: (202) 842-3490
e-mail: cato@cato.org
Web site: www.cato.org

This libertarian public policy research foundation supports limited government, individual liberty, free markets, and peace. It publishes the quarterly *Cato Journal.* One of its books is *It's Getting Better All the Time: 100 Greatest Trends of the Last 100 Years,* available on its Web site.

Center for the Study of Urban Poverty (CSUP)
UCLA—Institute for Social Science Research
  Los Angeles, CA   90095-1484
(310) 825-9156 • fax: (310) 206-4472
email: ofeliac@csrs.ucla.edu

Web site: www.sscnet.ucla.edu/issr/csup/index.php

The center's mission is to research the causes and consequences of urban poverty. It focuses on poverty in Los Angeles, the working poor, and transitioning low-skill and disadvantaged workers into the labor market. It publishes working papers and policy briefs, which are available on its Web site.

Center of Concern

1225 Otis St. NE, Washington, DC   20017
(202) 635-2757 • fax: (202) 832-9494
e-mail: coc@coc.org
Web site: www.coc.org

The center engages in social analysis, theological reflection, policy advocacy, and public education on issues of justice and peace. It seeks to end hunger, poverty, environmental decline, and injustice in the United States and worldwide. It publishes *Center Focus,* its quarterly newsletter, as well as numerous articles, papers, and press releases.

Economic Policy Institute (EPI)

1660 L St. NW, Suite 1200, Washington, DC   20036
(202) 775-8810 • fax: (202) 775-0819
email: epi@epi.org
Web site: www.epi.org

The institute seeks to promote a prosperous, fair, and sustainable economy. It researches living standards and labor markets, government and the economy, globalization and trade, education, and retirement policy. EPI publishes books, studies, issue briefs, and education materials, most of which are available on its Web site.

Galen Institute

PO Box 19080, Alexandria, VA   22320
(703) 299-8900 • fax: (703) 299-0721
e-mail: galen@galen.org
Web site: www.galen.org

The institute is a free-market research organization devoted exclusively to health policy. It believes that a consumer-driven market will lower costs, promote innovation, expand choice, and increase access to better medical care. Its Web site offers a weekly newsletter, *Health Policy Matters,* as well as press releases and articles.

Heartland Institute
19 S. LaSalle St., Suite 903
   Chicago, IL   60603
(312) 377-4000
e-mail: think@heartland.org
Web site: www.heartland.org

The Heartland Institute focuses on education, health care, and the environment. It is a libertarian think tank that believes in empowering people with the principles of individual rights and limited government. It publishes the *Heartlander* and *Health Care News.*

The Heritage Foundation
214 Massachusetts Ave. NE
   Washington, DC   20002-4999
(202) 546-4400 • fax: (202) 546-8328
e-mail: info@heritage.org
Web site: www.heritage.org

The mission of this think tank is to formulate and promote conservative public policies based on the principles of free enterprise, limited government, individual freedom, traditional American values, and a strong national defense. Its Web site offers analysis on current policy issues, access to conservative experts, key economic figures, and to the *Insider,* a quarterly publication.

Institute for Research on Poverty (IRP)
1180 Observatory Dr., Madison, WI   53706
e-mail: irpweb@ssc.wisc.edu
Web site: www.irp.wisc.edu

IRP is based at the University of Wisconsin–Madison. It researches the causes and consequences of poverty and social inequality in the United States. Its Web site offers reports and its newsletter, *Focus.*

International Fund for Agricultural Development (IFAD)

Via del Serafico, 107, 00142
  Rome 39-065459 Italy
fax: +39 06 5043463
e-mail: ifad@ifad.org
Web site: www.ifad.org

The mission of IFAD is to enable the rural poor to overcome poverty. It operates in 115 countries and territories to improve quality of life. Photos, videos, fact sheets, reports, and other documents are available on its Web site.

National Student Campaign Against Hunger and Homelessness (NSCAHH)

233 N. Pleasant St., Suite 32
  Amherst, MA   01002
(413) 253-6417 • fax: (413) 256-6435
email: info@studentsagainsthunger.org
Web site: www.nscahh.org

NSCAHH is a network of college and high school students, educators, and community leaders fighting to end hunger and homelessness in the United States and abroad. It seeks to create student and community activists who will explore and understand the root causes of poverty and initiate positive change through service and action. It offers training and on-site visits for activists, reports on hunger and homelessness, and a recommended reading list.

Oxfam International

26 West St., Boston, MA   02111-1206
(617) 482-1211 • fax: (617) 728-2594
e-mail: info@oxfamamerica.org
Web site: www.oxfam.org

Oxfam International is a group of twelve organizations working together with over three thousand partners in more than one hundred countries to find lasting solutions to poverty, suffering, and injustice. It focuses on issues such as education, gender, HIV/AIDS, and human rights. Its Web site offers news, policy analysis, and press releases.

Population Reference Bureau (PRB)
1875 Connecticut Ave. NW, Suite 520
   Washington, DC   20009-5728
(800) 877-9881 • fax: (202) 328-3937
e-mail: popref@prb.org
Web site: www.prb.org

PRB informs people about the population dimensions of important social, economic, and political issues. It publishes the quarterly *Population Bulletin,* the annual *World Population Data Sheet,* and *PRB Reports on America.*

Rural Poverty Research Center (RPRC)
Oregon State University
   Corvallis, OR   97331-3601
(541) 737-1442 • fax: (541) 737-2563
e-mail: rprc@oregonstate.edu
Web site: www.rprconline.org

RPRC is part of the Rural Policy Research Institute. RPRC works to create a national dialogue within the poverty research, policy, and practitioner community with the aim of creating an integrated rural poverty research agenda. It publishes working papers and research briefs. Its Web site offers a map of persistent poverty counties in the United States.

Bibliography

Books

Heather Boushey et al.

Hardships in America. Washington, DC: Economic Policy Institute, 2001; Berkeley and Los Angeles: University of California Press, 2003.

Samuel Casey Carter

No Excuses: Lessons from 21 High-Performing, High-Poverty Schools. Washington, DC: Heritage Foundation, 2000.

Mona Charen

Do-Gooders: How Liberals Hurt Those They Claim to Help (and the Rest of Us). New York: Sentinel, 2004.

Robert Guest

The Shackled Continent: Power, Corruption, and African Lives. London: Macmillan, 2004.

Chester Hartman, ed.

Challenges to Equality: Poverty and Race in America. Armonk, NY: M.E. Sharpe, 2001.

Jack M. Hollander

The Real Environmental Crisis: Why Poverty, Not Affluence, Is the Environment's Number One Enemy. Berkeley and Los Angeles: University of California Press, 2003.

Robert A. Isaak

The Globalization Gap: How the Rich Get Richer and the Poor Get Left Further Behind. Upper Saddle River, NJ: Prentice-Hall/Financial Times, 2005.

Michael Johnston

In the Deep Heart's Core. New York: Grove Press, 2002.

Michelle Kennedy

Without a Net: Middle Class and Homeless (with Kids) in America; My Story. New York: Viking, 2005.

Walter Laqueur

No End to War: Terrorism in the Twenty-First Century. New York: Continuum International, 2003.

Robert H. Lauer and Jeannette C. Lauer

Troubled Times: Readings in Social Problems. Los Angeles: Roxbury, 2000.

Sar A. Levitan et al.

Programs in Aid of the Poor. 8th ed. Baltimore: Johns Hopkins University Press, 2003.

Gary MacDougal

Make a Difference: How One Man Helped Solve America's Poverty Problem. New York: Truman Talley Books/St. Martin's Press, 2000.

Garth L. Mangum, Stephen L. Mangum, and Andrew M. Sum

The Persistence of Poverty in the United States. Baltimore: Johns Hopkins University Press, 2003.

Paul Milbourne

Rural Poverty: Marginalisation and Exclusion in Britain and the United States. New York: Routledge, 2004.

Stephen Moore and Julian L. Simon

It's Getting Better All the Time: 100 Greatest Trends of the Last 100 Years. Washington, DC: Cato Institute, 2000.

| Deepa Narayan et al. | *Voices of the Poor.* Vol. 2: *Crying Out for Change.* New York: Oxford University Press, 2000. |

Deepa Narayan and Patti Petesch, eds.
Voices of the Poor. Vol. 3: *From Many Lands.* New York: Oxford University Press, 2002.

Benjamin L. Page and James R. Simmons
What Government Can Do: Dealing with Poverty and Inequality. Chicago: University of Chicago Press, 2000.

Mark Robert Rank
One Nation, Underprivileged: Why American Poverty Affects Us All. New York: Oxford University Press, 2004.

Maria Ressa
Seeds of Terror: An Eyewitness Account of Al-Qaeda's Newest Center of Operations in Southeast Asia. New York: Free Press, 2003.

Loretta Schwartz-Nobel
Growing Up Empty: The Hunger Epidemic in America. New York: HarperCollins, 2002.

David K. Shipler
The Working Poor: Invisible in America. New York: Knopf, 2004.

Thomas Sowell
Applied Economics: Thinking Beyond Stage One. New York: Basic Books, 2004.

Periodicals

Alberto Abadie
"Poverty, Political Freedom, and the Roots of Terrorism," Working Paper no.

W10859, National Bureau of Economic Research, October 2004.

Ronald Bailey — "Free Market Health Care," *Reason Online,* March 28, 2003. www.reason.com/rb/rb052803.shtml.

Ronald Bailey — "The Nature of Poverty," *Reason Online,* July 13, 2005. http://www.reason.com/rb/rb071305.shtml.

David E. Bloom, David Canning, and Dean T. Jamison — "Health, Wealth, and Welfare," *Finance Development,* March 2004.

Kevin Carey — "The Real Value of Teachers," *Thinking K-16,* vol. 8, no. 1, Winter 2004.

Center on Hunger and Poverty — "The Consequences of Hunger and Food Insecurity for Children," June 2002. www.centeronhunger.org/pdf/ConsequencesofHunger.pdf.

Center on Hunger and Poverty — "The Paradox of Hunger and Obesity in America," July 2003. www.centeronhunger.org/pdf/hungerandobesity.pdf.

Shantayanan Devarajan and Ritva Reinikka — "Making Services Work for Poor People," *Finance & Development,* September 2003.

Jeanette Froehlich "Steps Toward Dismantling Poverty for Working, Poor Women," *Work,* vol. 24, no. 4, 2005.

Jessica Garrison "The Irresistible Force of a Teacher's Will," *Los Angeles Times,* April 21, 2002.

Peter G. Gosselin "How Just a Handful of Setbacks Sent the Ryans Tumbling Out of Prosperity," *Los Angeles Times,* December 30, 2004.

Peter G. Gosselin "If America Is Richer, Why Are Its Families So Much Less Secure?" *Los Angeles Times,* October 10, 2004.

Peter G. Gosselin "The Poor Have More Things Today— Including Wild Income Swings," *Los Angeles Times,* December 12, 2004.

Eugene Kane "Minimum Wage Just Not Enough," *Milwaukee Journal Sentinel Online,* January 8, 2005. http://www.jsonline.com/news/metro/jan05/291327.asp.

June Kronholz "Trying to Close the Stubborn Learning Gap," *Wall Street Journal,* August 19, 2003.

Carol Lancaster "Poverty, Terrorism, and National Security," Woodrow Wilson International Center for Scholars, August 8, 2003.

www.wilsoncenter.org/news/docs/
ACF59B4.doc.

Dan LeRoy "Rural Women on Welfare Facing Bleak Prospects," *Women's eNews,* May 27, 2001. www.womensenews.org/ article.cfm/dyn/aid/562.

Mike Lynch "Health Insurance: It's a Policy, Not a Choice," *Reason Online,* March 28, 2002. http://www.reason.com/ml/ ml032802.shtml.

George Monbiot "What Do We Really Want?" *Guardian,* August 27, 2002.

Evelyn Nieves "Forget Washington. The Poor Cope Alone," *New York Times,* September 26, 2000.

Michael Radu "The Futile Search for the 'Root Causes' of Terrorism," *Foreign Policy Research Institute E-Notes,* April 23, 2002. www.fpri.org/enotes/ americawar.20020423.radu.futilesearch forrootcauses.html.

RAND Health "Does Neighborhood Deterioration Lead to Poor Health?" RAND Research Brief RB-9074, 2005. www.rand.org/ publications/RB/RB9074/.

Martin Ravallion and Shaohua Chen "Understanding China's (Uneven) Progress Against Poverty," *Finance & Development,* December 2004.

Alan Reynolds   "School Voucher Venture," *Washington Times,* September 21, 2003.

Carla Rivera   "Plight of the Hotel Children," *Los Angeles Times,* September 7, 2004.

Geoffrey E. Schneider   "Globalization and the Poorest of the Poor: Global Integration and the Development Process in Sub-Saharan Africa," *Journal of Economic Issues,* vol. 37, no. 2, June 2003.

Stephanie Simon   "No Job, but Lots of Work," *Los Angeles Times,* January 17, 2003.

Stephanie Simon   "The Old South, Up North," *Los Angeles Times,* December 30, 2002.

Stephanie Simon   "Reaching for Rural Renewal," *Los Angeles Times,* July 2, 2002.

Stephanie Simon   "Tuition That Oinks," *Los Angeles Times,* November 13, 2002.

Thomas Sowell   "Wal-Mart's Obligation Is to Its Customers," *Charleston (S.C.) Daily Mail,* May 17, 2005.

Megan K. Stack   "A Healing Torturous as War," *Los Angeles Times,* June 1, 2004.

Laura D'Andrea Tyson   "For Developing Countries, Health Is Wealth," *Business Week,* January 14, 2002.

Gaia Vince

"Wealth Does Not Always Predict Health," *NewScientist.com,* July 22, 2005. www.newscientist.com/ article.ns?id=dn7712.

James D. Wolfensohn

"Fight Terrorism and Poverty," *Development Outreach,* Fall 2001.

Index